SHORTCUTS TO S

Business for Leaving Certificate

PADRAIG FITZPATRICK

GILL & MACMILLAN

Gill & Macmillan Ltd
Hume Avenue
Park West
Dublin 12
with associated companies throughout the world
www.gillmacmillan.ie

© Padraig Fitzpatrick 2007

978 0 7171 4170 8

Print origination by
Carrigboy Typesetting Services.

*The paper used in this book is made from the wood pulp of managed forests.
For every tree felled, at least one tree is planted, thereby renewing natural resources.*

CONTENTS

INTRODUCTION   vii

CHAPTER 1: *Unit 1: People in Business*   1

CHAPTER 2: *Unit 2: Enterprise*   16

CHAPTER 3: *Unit 3: Managing I*   21

CHAPTER 4: *Unit 4: Managing II*   49

CHAPTER 5: *Unit 5: Business in Action*   75

CHAPTER 6: *Unit 6: Domestic Environment*   100

CHAPTER 7: *Unit 7: The International Trading Environment*   133

CHAPTER 8: *Sample Applied Business Question*   150

To my wife, Loraine, for her help and support and our lovely son, Sean, who ensured I took regular breaks from my work.

INTRODUCTION

BUSINESS COURSE OUTLINE

The Leaving Certificate Business course consists of **seven** units. Each of these seven units is divided into a number of distinct sub-units. These units and sub-units correspond to the syllabus the Leaving Certificate papers are constructed from each year. Within each of these sub-units, material is presented under a number of headings, which are also taken from the syllabus.

Unit 1: Introduction to People in Business

1.1: People and their relationships in business
1.2: Conflicting interests and how they are resolved

Unit 2: Enterprise

2.1: Introduction and definition of enterprise
2.2: Entrepreneurs and enterprise skills

Unit 3: Managing I

3.1: Introduction and definition of management
3.2: Managers and management skills
3.3: Management activities

Unit 4: Managing II

4.1: Household and business manager
4.2: Human resource management
4.3: Changing role of management
4.4: Monitoring the business

Unit 5: Business in Action

5.1: Identifying opportunities
5.2: Marketing
5.3: Getting started
5.4: Expansion

Unit 6: Domestic Environment

6.1: Categories of industry
6.2: Types of business organisations
6.3: Community development
6.4: Business and the economy
6.5: Government and business
6.6: Social responsibilities of business

Unit 7: International Environment

7.1: Introduction to the international trading environment
7.2: European Union
7.3: International business

HIGHER LEVEL PAPER

Students **must** do section 1 (short questions) and section 2 (Applied Business Question). **One** question must be done from section 3 part 1, **two** questions must be done from section 3 part 2, and then a fourth question must be done from **either** part 1 or part 2. **Four** long questions in total must be answered.

> **Exam Tip:** The student is asked to answer eight short questions out of the ten given. However, you should always do **all ten** of the short questions. This allows you to make a mistake in a couple of your answers. Remember, only the best eight will count.

> **Exam Tip:** In the Applied Business Question (ABQ), always **read the ABQ question before reading the text.** Underline the requirement of the question. This then makes your reading of the text more meaningful. Ideally you should read the text separately for each of the questions given. Each point made should tie in to the text.

Timing for the exam

Every year I meet students coming out of the business exam commenting on how long the paper was and how impossible it was to get all the questions done in the three hours allotted (two and a half hours for Ordinary Level). Some do not even get a fourth question done. From the students' point of view, this must be disappointing and frustrating. However, what many of these students are really saying is that they spent too long on one or more of the questions.

Time management is an important part of the business exam, which usually requires a lot of writing. In fact, sometimes the difficulty for students is not that they do not know something, but rather, that they know an awful lot about a certain topic and must actually leave out some information in order to complete a question in a reasonable amount of time. Remember, it is possible to get maximum/very high marks in a question without going on and on. As such, this book is as much about exam preparation as a presentation of information.

At the end of each section I will present some exam/syllabus questions (remember, the exam questions are taken from the syllabus) with marks assigned to them and show you how to answer these questions based on the marks assigned. As you go through the book, you will learn what you need to do to get the maximum, or at least very high, marks in each question.

This book attempts to answer a very common question that many students ask: 'How much do I need to write?' The total time available is 180 minutes for 400 marks, which works out as follows:

10 mark question	4 minutes
15 mark question	6 minutes
20 mark question	8 minutes
30 mark question	12 minutes
40 mark question	16 minutes
60 mark question	24 minutes
80 mark question	32 minutes

This timing structure allows **twenty minutes** for reading the paper, thinking, jotting down notes or themes, etc. Also, a student could spend an extra couple of minutes on some questions if necessary. It is possible that many students will find that they are able to do the short questions in a bit less than thirty-two minutes. This time saving could then be transferred to the Applied Business Question, which many students feel takes a bit longer than the thirty-two minutes allowed. It would even be possible to spend forty or forty-five minutes on the ABQ. **Time discipline is very important.**

Ordinary Level Paper

Students must answer ten out of the fifteen short questions given in section 1. In part 1 of section 2, **one** question must be answered. **Two** questions must be answered from part 2. One question must be answered from **either** part 1 or part 2. **Four** long questions in total must be answered.

> **Exam Tip:** Although you are asked to do ten out of the fifteen short questions, you should always attempt to do **all fifteen** if possible, as this allows you to make a mistake in a couple of your answers. Remember, only the best ten will count.

Exam timing

The total time available for the Ordinary Level paper is 150 minutes for 400 marks. This works out as follows:

10 mark question	3.5 minutes
20 mark question	7 minutes
30 mark question	10 minutes
75 mark question	25 minutes
100 mark question	35 minutes

This allows approximately ten to fifteen minutes for reading the paper.

CHAPTER 1
Unit 1: People in Business

1.1: PEOPLE AND THEIR RELATIONSHIPS IN BUSINESS

STAKEHOLDERS IN BUSINESS

- **Producers/manufacturers:** Businesses that make the products and supply them to retailers or consumers. An example of a producer is Kerry Group PLC.
- **Consumers:** The people who buy goods and services for their own use. Good consumers will know their rights in the marketplace.
- **Employers:** People who hire other people to work for them in return for pay. Employers have certain responsibilities, e.g. to pay a fair wage and to have safe working conditions.
- **Employees:** People hired by the employer to do work in return for pay. They have certain rights, e.g. to be paid a fair wage (at least the minimum wage) and have safe working conditions.
- **Entrepreneurs:** People with the vision to set up a business. They come up with the idea and take a risk. Examples of Irish entrepreneurs are Brody Sweeney (O'Brien's Sandwich Bars) and Sean Quinn (Quinn Direct, Quinn Cement).
- **Investors:** Investors put money into a business in the hope of getting a good return. The investor usually gets part ownership in the new firm.
- **Service providers:** A service provider supplies a service to a business in order for it to run efficiently. Examples of service providers are the ESB, Bord Gáis, insurance companies, banks, etc.
- **Interest groups:** Organisations that protect and promote their members' interests by speaking on their behalf and lobbying for change for them. They are sometimes called pressure groups. An example is the Consumers Association of Ireland (CAI).
- **Local communities:** The areas and people around which business operates. Every community is affected in some way by business. Firms should listen to the concerns of the local community.

RELATIONSHIPS BETWEEN THE STAKEHOLDERS

- A co-operative relationship is one where the stakeholders make efforts to get on with each other, e.g. producers paying suppliers on time.
- A competitive relationship is one where the stakeholders are competing with each other, e.g. two businesses competing for customers.
- Conflict may arise between stakeholders, e.g. employers and employees, business and interest groups.

These relationships are **dynamic**, i.e. they can change over time. For instance, two firms may be in competition but help each other out on some issues, such as distribution.

Exam Tip: If you are asked to explain, describe or contrast the relationship between two stakeholders (as is frequently asked), then the best approach to take is to give a definition of each stakeholder, followed by a description of the relationship that might exist between them. See p. 4 for an example of this.

LAW OF CONTRACT

A contract is a legally binding agreement between two parties. A contract can be made orally, in writing or by conduct.

Elements of the law of contract

- **Offer:** An offer can be made orally, in writing or by conduct. An offer can be made by the seller offering to sell or the buyer offering to buy. An offer can be accepted, rejected or revoked. An **invitation to treat** is not an offer, but rather an offer to make an offer, e.g. goods displayed in a shop window are an invitation to treat.
- **Acceptance:** Acceptance can be made orally, in writing or by conduct. Acceptance must exactly match an offer, otherwise it is a **counteroffer**.
- **Consideration:** This is the **payment** that passes between the parties. Consideration must be real and have value, but it need not be adequate. This means that a car could be sold for €1 if the parties agreed to it. This is clearly not adequate, but at least it is real and has a value.
- **Capacity to contract:** A person must have the legal capacity to enter into a contract. The following do not have legal capacity to contract:
  - ➤ People under the age of eighteen.
  - ➤ People under the influence of drink or drugs.
  - ➤ People of unsound mind.
  - ➤ Company directors who act outside their powers (*ultra vires*).
- **Intention to contract:** People entering into a contract must have the intention of entering a legally binding agreement. An important point here is the separation of business agreements from personal ones.

- **Consent:** Both parties must consent to enter into the contract of their own free will and knowing all the important facts. If there is pressure put on one party by the other to enter into the contract, then there is no real consent.
- **Legal form:** Some contracts must be in a certain form in order to be legal, e.g. contracts for the sale of land and hire purchase contracts must be in writing.

Termination of the contract

A contract can be terminated (ended) in four ways:

- **Performance:** The contract is ended when both parties carry out their duties as agreed in the contract. For example, a promoter may hire a band to perform a concert at a certain venue for a set fee. The band plays at the concert and the promoter pays them. The contract has been performed by both parties and is therefore ended.
- **Agreement:** Both parties may agree to end the contract at any time, even though it may not have been performed. For example, in the above situation, the promoter and the band may jointly decide that since tickets are selling slowly it might be best to end the contract and cancel the concert.
- **Frustration:** This is where some unforeseen event happens that makes it impossible for the contract to be carried out. In the above example, if the concert venue was flooded on the date of the concert, then it would be impossible for the contract to be carried out.
- **Breach:** When one party does not perform their contractual duties as agreed, the contract is said to be breached (broken), e.g. if the band does not show up for the concert, they have breached the contract and can be sued by the promoter.

Remedies for breach of contract

Remedies depend on whether a condition or a warranty has been broken. A **condition** is an essential part of the contract, e.g. the band showing up for the concert itself. A **warranty** is a less serious part of the contract, e.g. the band doing a press conference to promote the concert.

- **Rescind (cancel) the contract:** If a condition is broken, the injured party can cancel the contract, i.e. refuse to honour it. In the example above, if the band did not show up for the actual concert, the promoter can cancel the contract and refuse to pay them anything. He/she could also sue the band for any losses or expenses incurred.
- **Sue for damages:** If a warranty is broken, the injured party can sue for losses incurred but cannot cancel the contract, e.g. if the band did not show up for a press conference to promote the concert and ticket sales suffered as a result, then the promoter could sue the band for loss of profit but could not actually cancel the contract.

- **Specific performance:** The courts may order that the terms of the contract be carried out as originally agreed, e.g. the court may order the band to perform the concert on a different date. The injured party may request this.

EXAM QUESTIONS

> ### Exam question 1
>
> *Describe the relationship that might exist between entrepreneurs and investors in a business.*
> (20 marks)
>
> ### Marking scheme
> Remember, you have approximately eight minutes to do this question. A marking scheme might be applied as follows:
>
> - Explain entrepreneur (**5 marks**).
> - Explain investor (**5 marks**).
> - Describe the relationship between them (**10 marks**). The ten marks might be split into two **5 marks** for two points.
>
> ### Sample answer
> An entrepreneur is a person who comes up with an idea for a new product or service. He/she then takes the risk and sets up a business to try and make money. (**5 marks**)
>
> An investor is a person or institution that invests money in the entrepreneur's venture. This may be a shareholder or a venture capital company. (**5 marks**)
>
> The relationship between the two will be a co-operative one to start with. The entrepreneur is happy to get the capital and the investor is hoping for a return on their investment. However, if the business fails to make any money and/or the investor feels that things are moving too slowly, the relationship may change to a competitive or conflicting one. For example, the investor may want a quicker return on the investment, while the entrepreneur wants more time. This could be called a dynamic relationship. (**10 marks**)

Exam question 2

Explain four methods by which a legal contract can be terminated. (20 marks)

Marking scheme

The marking scheme here is **four** points at **5 marks** each. The name gets **2 marks**, while the explanation gets **3 marks**.

Sample answer

- **Performance (2 marks):** When both parties to the contract perform their duties as agreed in the contract, the contract is terminated. **(3 marks)**
- **Agreement (2 marks):** A contract may be terminated if both parties to the contract agree to end it, even though it may not have been performed. **(3 marks)**
- **Frustration (2 marks):** If some event happens that makes it impossible to carry out the contract, then the contract is ended. **(3 marks)**
- **Breach (2 marks):** The contract may be ended if one of the parties involved in it does not carry out their duties as agreed. This breaks the contract. **(3 marks)**

In this case examples are unnecessary, as the question does not ask for them.

Exam Tip: Rewrite this answer for yourself. How did you do on time? Did you do it in eight minutes or less? How much did you write? These sample questions will become a guide for your timing and length of answers.

1.2: CONFLICTING INTERESTS AND HOW THEY ARE RESOLVED

The main areas of conflict in business are:
- Consumer–retailer conflict.
- Employer–employee conflict.

CONSUMER–RETAILER CONFLICT – NON-LEGISLATIVE RESOLUTION

- The consumer should first go back to the retailer, as the consumer's contract is with the retailer.
- If the consumer is not satisfied with this, then he/she should write a letter of complaint.
- If still not satisfied, the consumer should contact the seller's **trade association**, e.g. ITAA (Irish Travel Agents Association).
- Another option is the **Consumers Association of Ireland** (CAI). This organisation provides advice to consumers on their rights.

The Ombudsman

The job of the Ombudsman is to investigate complaints by members of the public who feel that they have been treated unfairly by an organisation. The Ombudsman is an independent third party. Individuals must have tried to solve the problem themselves before taking it to the Ombudsman. There are three types of Ombudsman at present:

- **Ombudsman for state agencies:** Deals with complaints about state-owned companies. It issues recommendations, which are not binding.
- **Financial services Ombudsman:** Hears complaints concerning banks/building societies. The individual has a right to accept or reject the decision.
- **Ombudsman for the insurance industry:** Investigates complaints against insurance companies. The member insurance companies agree to be bound by its decisions, but the individual can reject the Ombudsman's decision.

CONSUMER–RETAILER CONFLICT – LEGISLATIVE RESOLUTION

Sale of Goods and Supply of Services Act 1980

The main provisions of this Act are as follows.

- **Responsibility:** The retailer is the person responsible for defects, even if it is the manufacturer's fault, as the contract is with the seller.
- **Goods:** Goods must be of merchantable quality, fit for their purpose, match their description and match their sample if sold by sample.
- **Services:** The seller must have the necessary skill to provide the service and must provide it with care. Any materials used in the service must be fit for their purpose and goods supplied with the service should be of merchantable quality.
- **Redress:** Redress depends on how serious the fault is and how soon the consumer complained. Redress can be a repair, replacement or a refund (the three Rs). If a complaint is valid, a credit note need not be accepted.
- **Unsolicited goods:** It is an offence for a seller to demand payment for unsolicited goods. The consumer may keep these goods if six months have passed and the seller has not collected them, or if thirty days have passed since the customer told the seller he/she did not want them and they have not been collected.
- **Guarantees** provided by manufacturers or retailers are additional benefits and do not replace customers' usual statutory rights.
- **Hire purchase:** Consumers renting goods or buying them on hire purchase have the exact same rights as those who buy them for cash or on credit.

Consumer Information Act 1978

The main provisions of this Act are as follows.

- **Purpose:** To protect consumers against false or misleading claims about goods' services and prices.
- **Goods:** It is an offence for a seller to give false or misleading information about goods. It is an offence to apply a false trade description to goods, e.g. 'Made in Ireland' if it is not made in Ireland.
- **Services:** The Act prohibits false or misleading information about services, e.g. 'one-hour photo' which takes more than one hour.
- **Prices:** The Act prohibits false or misleading information about the price, previous price or the recommended price of goods or services.
- **Sales:** It is an offence to give a false or misleading indication of a previous price. Goods on sale must have been at the higher price for at least twenty-eight consecutive days in the previous three months.
- **Advertising:** The Act prohibits false or misleading claims about goods or services. It is forbidden to publish any ad that is likely to cause loss, damage or injury to members of the public.
- **The Office of the Director of Consumer Affairs** was set up under this Act. The role of the Director is to ensure that the Acts are being complied with.

Director of Consumer Affairs

This is the state agency that ensures that businesses are complying with consumer legislation. Its functions are:

- To ensure firms are **complying** with the Consumer Information Act and the Sale of Goods and Supply of Services Act.
- To **promote high standards** in advertising.
- To request the **alteration or cessation** of an advertisement that is false, misleading or offensive to members of the public.
- To **investigate complaints** made by members of the public. The Director has the power to **prosecute** offenders.
- The Director **monitors EU legislation** and ensures Irish firms are complying with it.
- The Director prepares an annual report and **advises** the government on consumer affairs issues.

Small Claims Court

This is where consumers can take their case if they cannot resolve it with the retailer. The two main advantages of the Small Claims Court are that it is **inexpensive** and offers a **quick** resolution. The consumer pays a fee of €9 to the court and has their case heard. The court can award compensation up to a maximum of €1270. The court cannot enforce a judgment, but the majority of its recommendations are accepted.

EMPLOYER–EMPLOYEE CONFLICT – NON-LEGISLATIVE RESOLUTION

- An atmosphere of open communication, consultation and discussion in the workplace will reduce conflict.
- The employee can take their complaint to the **shop steward**. This is the employee who is elected to be the workers' representative.
- The shop steward will meet with the **human resources manager**. A **code of practice** will be followed.
- A representative from the **trade union head office** may meet the employers' union, the Irish Business and Employers Confederation (IBEC).

If at this stage the dispute is not resolved, the parties involved may seek the help of an outside agency.

Industrial relations

Industrial relations refers to the relationship that exists between employers and employees in a business.

TABLE 1.1: INDUSTRIAL RELATIONS

GOOD INDUSTRIAL RELATIONS	POOR INDUSTRIAL RELATIONS
Good morale, which means staff will be happy to be at work.	Low morale, which will lead to a poor atmosphere.
There will be lower labour turnover and absenteeism, as workers are happier to be at work.	Workers will leave jobs to find work elsewhere and will miss workdays. This will affect productivity.
Due to good relations in the workplace, the firm will have a good public image.	The public image of the firm will be affected and sales will fall.
An atmosphere of open and honest communication will prevail.	There will be a lack of trust and a hostile atmosphere between staff and management.
	Workers may take industrial action such as strikes.

Trade unions

Trade unions are organisations that represent the interests of employees by speaking and negotiating on their behalf with employers.

What do trade unions do for members?

- Trade unions **protect** workers' rights. They fight for better pay and working conditions, e.g. a shorter working week.
- They **negotiate** on behalf of workers with the government and employers' groups (IBEC) on national pay agreements.
- Trade unions provide **advice** to their members on industrial relations issues and on their rights in the workplace.
- Trade unions provide a sense of **solidarity** for workers. Individually, workers are weak. As a group, however, the union has a strong voice.
- Trade unions provide a sense of **job security** for workers.

Examples of trade unions are the Services, Industrial, Professional and Technical Union (SIPTU), Mandate, the Irish Nurses Organisation (INO) and the Association of Secondary Teachers in Ireland (ASTI).

EMPLOYER–EMPLOYEE CONFLICT – LEGISLATIVE RESOLUTION

Industrial Relations Act 1990

The main provisions of the Act are as follows.

- **Immunity:** Trade unions and workers are immune from legal action by the employers as a result of loss of profits arising out of a strike provided it is an official trade dispute and a secret ballot was held by the union before the strike action.
- **Picketing:** Peaceful picketing of the employer's premises is allowed. The strikers must keep moving and there must be no obstruction or intimidation of members of the public. Secondary picketing is also legal, but only if the picketers believe that the second employer is directly assisting the first in order to frustrate the industrial action.
- **Secret ballot:** A secret ballot must be held before any industrial action is taken. Every trade union must have a secret ballot included in its rules.
- **Trade disputes:** A trade dispute is defined as any dispute between employers and workers that is connected with the terms or conditions affecting any person at work.
- **Legitimate trade disputes** are ones connected with pay and conditions of work, dismissal/suspension of workers, trade union recognition or discrimination in the workplace.
- **Minimum notice:** Under the Act, the union must give the employer at least one week's notice of the intention to strike.

Labour Relations Commission (LRC)

The LRC was set up under the Industrial Relations Act 1990. Its duties include the following.

- Provides a **conciliation** service. This involves an **Industrial Relations Officer** (IRO) mediating between the two parties. The IRO makes a recommendation, which may be accepted or rejected.
- Provides **Rights Commissioners** who investigate disputes involving one person or a small group of workers on issues such as unfair dismissal, maternity leave, etc. They make recommendations, which may be accepted or rejected.
- Provides **codes of practice**. These are accepted procedures to deal with industrial relations problems. They are not legally binding, but consideration should be given to them.
- Provides an industrial relations **advisory service**. This is aimed at helping employers and employees to build a good industrial relations climate.
- Assists **Joint Labour Committees (JLCs)** and **Joint Industrial Councils (JICs)**. JLCs set minimum rates of pay for workers in their industry. JICs provide harmonious relations in their industry.
- Conducts **research** into and monitors developments in industrial relations matters.

Labour Court

The Labour Court is generally considered the **court of last resort**. A sitting of the Labour Court involves an independent chairperson, an employer representative and an employee representative. Witnesses may be summoned to give evidence.

Functions of the Labour Court:
- It **investigates disputes** in certain circumstances:
  - ➤ On appeal from the LRC.
  - ➤ If the LRC has waived its right to be involved.
  - ➤ If there are exceptional circumstances.
  - ➤ If the Minister for Enterprise, Trade and Employment requests it.
- The Labour Court **interprets codes of practice**. It also **investigates breaches** of these codes of practice.
- It hears **appeals** on decisions made by Rights Commissioners.
- It sets up **Joint Labour Committees** (which investigate pay and conditions) and makes **Employment Regulation Orders** giving legal effect to their proposals.
- It **registers agreements** between employers and employees.

Unfair Dismissals Act 1977–1993

This Act applies to anyone in continuous employment for one year and who is aged between sixteen and sixty-six and working at least eight hours per week. The main provisions are as follows.

- **Unfair dismissals** are those which are made on the grounds of pregnancy, race, membership of the Travelling community, membership of a trade union or being involved in a strike, sexual orientation, religious or political beliefs, gender, marital status or colour.
- **Dismissals regarded as fair** are those involving incompetence of the worker, lack of qualifications, misconduct or redundancy due to economic conditions.
- **The burden of proof** will be on the employer to prove that the dismissal was fair and not on the employee to prove that it was unfair.
- **Constructive dismissal** is illegal. This is where the employer makes life so difficult for the employee that he/she is forced to leave. The employee has the same rights in this case as if they were dismissed directly.
- **Proper procedure:** The employee must be made aware of the problems with his/her performance. Efforts to resolve them must be made. Employers must give both oral and written warnings to the employee before dismissing him/her.
- All employees have certain **entitlements**. They should know the reason for the dismissal, have the right to reply to it and have the right to an impartial hearing.
- A worker who has been dismissed can appeal to a **Rights Commissioner,** and if unhappy with the decision, then to the **Employment Appeals Tribunal (EAT)**. Alternatively, a worker can go directly to the EAT.
- **Redress:** If the worker wins their case, he/she may be reinstated to their old position, be re-engaged in the original job or in another job under acceptable conditions or receive compensation of up to two years' wages.

Employment Equality Act 1998

- The Act **defined discrimination** as the *'treatment of one person in a less favourable way than another person is, has been or would be treated'*. Discrimination is illegal on nine distinct grounds: gender, marital status, family status, sexual orientation, religious belief, age, disability, race or membership of the Travelling community.
- **Harassment:** Both harassment in general and sexual harassment in particular were defined and outlawed under the Act. Harassment is defined as *'any behaviour which is unwelcome and offensive no matter what form it takes'*.
- **Equal pay:** All employment contracts must have an equal pay clause which states that all employees are entitled to equal pay for like work. Like work means the same work, similar work or work of equal value.

- **Equality Authority:** The Equality Authority was set up under the Act. Its role is to:
  - ➤ Work towards the elimination of discrimination.
  - ➤ Promote equality of opportunity in employment.
  - ➤ Provide information to the public.
  - ➤ Monitor and review the operation of the Act.
- **Director of Equality Investigations:** Anyone who feels discriminated against can apply to the Director. He decides whether these cases should be examined by an **Equality Mediation Officer**, who deals with them in a conciliatory manner, or by an **Equality Officer**, who will follow a more formal approach. The Director makes a final decision, which can be appealed to the Labour Court within forty-two days.
- **Redress:** The Director of Equality Investigations may order one of the following:
  - ➤ Equal **pay and arrears** for a period not exceeding three years to be paid in equal pay cases.
  - ➤ Equality treatment and **compensation** up to a maximum of two years' pay to be given in all other cases.

Data Protection Act 1988

This Act applies to personal information held about individuals on computer.

Rights of data subjects

- **Access to files:** A person on whom information is held has a right to get a copy of that data within forty days of making a written request.
- **Correction of errors:** A person has a right to have any errors or inaccurate information corrected or removed from file.
- A person has a **right to complain** to the Data Protection Commissioner.
- A person may claim **compensation** if they feel that they have suffered as a result of inaccurate information being held about them.

Obligations/responsibilities of data controllers

- To obtain the information in an **accurate and lawful manner**.
- To use the information only for the **purpose** for which it was collected.
- The information must be kept **safe** and secure from any unauthorised access.
- A **copy** of the data must be provided to the data subject if requested.
- The information should only be **retained** for as long as is necessary.
- The data should be kept **accurate** and up to date.

Role/functions of the Data Protection Commissioner

- Maintains a **register** of data controllers.
- Prepares and publishes **codes of practice** in the area of data collection and storage.

- Issues **Enforcement Notices** to those who are in breach of the Act. This forces data controllers to correct or delete information.
- **Investigates complaints** made by data subjects about breaches of the Act.
- Issues **Prohibition Notices**, which prohibit the transfer of personal data outside the country.
- Gives **advice** and information to members of the public.

Exam Tip: In relation to the Acts and the organisations, learn the **recall words** in bold. This should make constructing your point easier.

You may also be being asked to write about **component parts** of the Acts or organisations. Examples of this are the Rights Commissioner, Data Protection Commissioner, Director of Equality Investigations, reasons for legitimate trade disputes, unfair grounds for dismissal and fair grounds for dismissal.

EXAM QUESTIONS

Exam question 1

Illustrate your understanding of the term 'conciliation'. (10 marks)

Marking scheme
This type of question generally requires two good pieces of information, probably at **5 marks** each (although it could be **6 marks** and **4 marks** or vice versa. The first mark is given for the first piece of information).

Sample answer
This is when an independent third party listens to both sides in a dispute and makes a recommendation. (**5 marks**) This recommendation does not have to be accepted by the parties. (**5 marks**)

Exam question 2

Evaluate how effective the main provisions of the Sale of Goods and Supply of Services Act 1980 are in protecting consumers. (25 marks)

Marking scheme
This is a straightforward **five** points at **5 marks** each. The marks are split into **2 marks** for naming/introducing the point and **3 marks** for developing it.

Sample answer

- **Responsibility (2 marks):** The responsibility for dealing with complaints rests with the retailer. The consumer's contract is with the retailer and not the manufacturer. **(3 marks)**
- **Goods (2 marks):** Goods must be of merchantable quality, fit for their purpose, match their description and match their sample. **(3 marks)**
- **Services (2 marks):** Services must be carried out by skilled people. They must use due care. Any spare parts used in the service must be of merchantable quality. **(3 marks)**
- **Redress (2 marks):** Redress may be a repair, replacement or refund. If the complaint is genuine, the consumer need not accept a credit note. **(3 marks)**
- **Unsolicited goods (2 marks):** A seller cannot demand payment for unsolicited goods. If the receiver of the goods indicates to the seller that he/she does not want the goods and the sender does not collect them, then after six months the receiver can keep them. **(3 marks)**

Exam question 3

Outline the role of the Labour Court in dealing with Irish industrial relations disputes. (20 marks)

Marking scheme

A typical marking scheme for this question would be **four** points at **5 marks** each. With a question like this, the student will not know whether the scheme is looking for four points at 5 marks each, or five points at 4 marks each. This is an understandable doubt, and sometimes the safest thing to do is to assume that the greater number of points is required. However, in this case, five roles/functions of the Labour Court would probably be a bit too demanding, so four points at 5 marks is the marking scheme.

Sample answer

- It investigates disputes in certain circumstances. **(2 marks)** These disputes might be sent to it on appeal from the LRC, if there are exceptional circumstances or if the Minister for Enterprise, Trade and Employment refers a case to it. **(3 marks)**
- The Labour Court interprets codes of practice. **(2 marks)** It also investigates breaches of codes of practice. It makes a decision, which is then binding. **(3 marks)**
- It hears appeals **(2 marks)** on decisions referred to it. These may be appeals on decisions made by Industrial Relations Officers or Rights Commissioners. **(3 marks)**
- It sets up Joint Labour Committees **(2 marks)** to investigate terms and conditions of lower-paid workers and makes Employment Regulation Orders to make them legal. **(3 marks)**

Important definitions from Unit 1

- **Stakeholder:** A person or organisation that is affected in some way by a business. These include customers, suppliers, interest groups, etc.
- **Contract:** A legally binding agreement between two parties. It can be made orally, in writing or by conduct.
- **Consideration:** The payment that takes place in a contract, e.g. John agrees to buy a car from Tom for €15,000. The consideration is the €15,000.
- **Invitation to treat:** This is not an offer, but rather an offer to make an offer, e.g. goods for sale in a shop window.
- **Capacity to contract:** The legal ability of a person to enter into a contract. If a person is under eighteen, of unsound mind or under the influence of alcohol or drugs, then they do not have legal capacity.
- **Specific performance:** When a contract is breached, the injured party can apply to the courts to get the party who has broken the contract to do what was agreed in the contract.
- **Condition:** A fundamental part of the contract. If a condition is broken, the injured party can cancel the entire contract.
- **Warranty:** A less important part of the contract. If a warranty is broken, the injured party cannot cancel the contract, but can sue for any losses.
- **Unsolicited goods:** Goods sent to a customer that have not been requested. If they have not been collected after six months, the customer may keep them.
- **Industrial relations:** The relationship that exists between employers and employees in the workplace.
- **Shop steward:** The union official elected by the workers to represent them. He/she provides information to the workers and negotiates with management on their behalf.
- **Conciliation:** When a third party tries to solve a workplace dispute. The recommendation of the third party, e.g. Industrial Relations Officer, does not have to be accepted.
- **Arbitration:** When a third party in the dispute makes a decision that the parties have agreed in advance to accept, e.g. a Labour Court decision on appeal.
- **Trade dispute:** Any dispute between employers and employees that is connected with the terms or conditions affecting any person at work.
- **Code of practice:** A set of agreed rules to be followed in the event of a dispute in the workplace. They are drawn up by the Labour Relations Commission.
- **Constructive dismissal:** This is where the employer makes life so difficult for the employee that he/she has no option but to leave. The employee can take a case for unfair dismissal.
- **Discrimination:** The treatment of one person in a less favourable way than another person is, has been or would be treated.
- **Data subject:** The person about whom data is collected and stored on computer. This person has certain rights under the Data Protection Act.
- **Data controller:** The person who holds and controls data on individuals on computer. This person has certain responsibilities under the Data Protection Act.

CHAPTER 2
Unit 2: Enterprise

Enterprise is the ability of an individual to recognise an opportunity and willingness to take the chance so that the opportunity will not be missed.

Examples of Irish **entrepreneurs** include Sean Quinn (Quinn Direct, Quinn Cement) and Pat McDonagh (Supermacs).

Intrapreneurs are employees who use their initiative and are enterprising within a business.

EXAMPLES OF ENTERPRISE

In the home:
- Doing some DIY around the house, e.g. tiling the bathroom.
- Converting the attic into an extra bedroom.

In business start-ups:
- Setting up a niche business, e.g. house-to-house IT maintenance.
- Using ideas from abroad, e.g. cafés and coffee bars.

In existing business:
- Installing an electronic stock control system.
- Developing a website to advertise and sell online.

In public life:
- The tax on plastic bags has reduced litter.
- The Irish government was one of the first in the world to ban smoking in public places.
- Urban renewal schemes have regenerated urban areas.

In the community:

- Many people are involved in sports clubs in their communities.
- Most towns and villages are involved in the Tidy Towns scheme.

At work:

- An employee might come up with an idea on how to speed up customers going through a check-out.
- A factory worker may have an idea that cuts down on waste material.

WHY PEOPLE BECOME ENTREPRENEURS

- **To make money:** Entrepreneurs feel they can make more money than they would if they were working for somebody else.
- **Independence:** They want to be their own boss and make their own decisions.
- **A challenge:** A person may feel more challenged by going it alone.
- **Family tradition:** For some people it has been a family tradition to set up their own business.
- **Free to follow their own values:** Some people feel they can put their beliefs into action by setting up a business.

CHARACTERISTICS OF ENTREPRENEURS

- **Creative and innovative:** They are always looking for new ideas and better ways to do things. Their creative streak allows them to come up with new ideas.
- **Decisive:** Most entrepreneurs can make quick decisions when the need arises. They can also make tough decisions that may not always be popular.
- **Flexible:** It is important that entrepreneurs are able to change their plans quickly as circumstances change.
- **Hard-working and energetic:** Behind every successful entrepreneur is a very hard-working person. Most of them put in long hours to get their projects off the ground.
- **Leaders:** Entrepreneurs need to have leadership qualities in order to get people to work with them. They are often **charismatic** people.
- **Realistic:** Entrepreneurs are realistic about what can be achieved and see things as they really are and not as they would like them to be. They also seek help from others when needed.
- **Resilient:** Entrepreneurs are very determined and motivated to succeed. When they encounter setbacks, they bounce back from them and learn from their mistakes.
- **Risk-takers:** Entrepreneurs are prepared to take personal and financial risks in a business venture. The risks they take are calculated ones.
- **Self-confident:** Entrepreneurs believe in their own ability and are confident that they can turn their ideas into successes. This is essential, as they may have many setbacks along the way.

ENTERPRISE SKILLS

- **Decision-making:** This involves making the best decisions as opposed to making quick ones. All the options are weighed up and the best one is chosen.
- **Human relations:** Entrepreneurs should be good at dealing with people. They come in contact with many stakeholders and need to have good communication skills to deal with them.
- **Inner control:** Entrepreneurs believe that they can influence events and make things happen. They don't believe in fate. They take charge of their own destiny.
- **Innovation skills:** Whereas this can be a characteristic, an entrepreneur can also learn to try new things. Idea generation is an area that entrepreneurs can give time and attention to.
- **Leadership skills:** Entrepreneurs need to be leaders to influence others about their way of thinking. This will enable them to motivate others around them.
- **Planning and goal setting:** Enterprising people believe in planning ahead and setting goals and targets. Nothing is left to chance.
- **Reality perception:** The entrepreneur must learn to see situations as they are. A common sense approach is essential rather than an emotional one.
- **Risk management:** Risk-taking is a characteristic, but risk management is a skill that can be learned. It involves getting as much information as possible and then making a calculated choice.
- **Time management:** This involves completing tasks within the allotted time and eliminating any activities that waste time. Prioritising is an important part of time management.

Exam Tip: It is unlikely that you will be asked for any more than **five** of either the skills or characteristics.

EXAM QUESTIONS

Exam question 1

Illustrate your understanding of the term 'intrapreneur'. (10 marks)

Marking scheme
As a short question, this is a 10 mark question. Generally, **two** good pieces of information are required at **5 marks** each. An example of intrapreneurship would probably be acceptable for one of the 5 marks.

Sample answer

An intrapreneur is an employee who is enterprising within a business. **(5 marks)** He/she comes up with suggestions as to how a firm may be able to improve its products or services or do something in an improved way. **(5 marks)**

Exam question 2

Identify the personal characteristics normally associated with entrepreneurial businesspeople. (20 marks)

Marking scheme

The scheme would be **five** points at **4 marks** each. The 4 marks would be split into **2 marks** for naming the entrepreneurial characteristic and **2 marks** for a piece of information on the characteristic. Examples could also be used to get the second 2 marks.

Sample answer

- **Creative and innovative (2 marks):** The entrepreneur is a creative thinker and comes up with new and interesting ideas for new goods and services. **(2 marks)**
- **Decisive (2 marks):** In order to take advantage of new ideas, the entrepreneur must be decisive and be prepared to act quickly before someone else comes up with a similar idea. **(2 marks)**
- **Hard-working (2 marks):** Behind most successful entrepreneurs is a very hard-working person. Long hours have to be put into the project to get it off the ground. **(2 marks)**
- **Realistic (2 marks):** Entrepreneurs have to see things as they really are and not as they would like them to be. They have to know their limitations. **(2 marks)**
- **Risk-takers (2 marks):** They take personal and financial risks, often with a high risk of failure. **(2 marks)**

IMPORTANT DEFINITIONS FROM UNIT 2

- **Enterprise:** A person's ability to recognise an opportunity and willingness to take a chance so that the opportunity will not be missed.
- **Entrepreneur:** A person who comes up with an idea for a business and takes the risk of setting up the business in the hope of making a profit.
- **Intrapreneur:** An employee who is enterprising in the place where he/she works. He/she comes up with ideas for new products or services or ways in which the firm may save money. Many firms promote intrapreneurship.

CHAPTER 3
Unit 3: Managing I

3.1: INTRODUCTION AND DEFINITION OF MANAGEMENT

Management is the process of directing human activities and physical resources towards achieving predetermined objectives.

TABLE 3.1: MANAGEMENT SKILLS AND ACTIVITIES

MANAGEMENT SKILLS	MANAGEMENT ACTIVITIES
Leading Motivating Communicating	Planning Organising Controlling

MANAGEMENT IN THE HOME

Holidays, school, family events, etc. must be **planned**. Children must be **organised** for school and family members must be organised to do household tasks. Household finances must be **controlled**. Budgets must be drawn up. Parents must show **leadership** to the children and **motivate** them to do schoolwork and work around the house. Good **communication** must take place between the family members.

MANAGEMENT IN BUSINESS

Managers must **plan** for the future of the business. This will involve both long- and short-term plans. The business must be **organised** properly. An organisational structure must exist in the business so that staff and management know their roles. Good **control** is also essential for the smooth running of the firm. This includes stock, credit and quality control. Managers must show **leadership** to staff and also **motivate** them properly.

Communication is essential in business, both within the business and between the business and its stakeholders.

MANAGEMENT IN SCHOOL

The management must **plan** timetables for teachers and students. Various events in the school year must be planned. Students must be **organised** into classes. School events must be organised. Various controls must be put in place. The school must work to a budget, so financial **control** is important. School principals must show **leadership** to teachers and students, and teachers must show leadership to students and try to **motivate** them. **Communication** is vital between management and staff and between teaching staff and students.

MANAGEMENT IN PUBLIC LIFE

Public services such as roads, schools, hospitals, libraries, parks, etc. must be **planned** well in advance. Each government department and local authority has to be **organised** with correct staffing levels and structures in place. **Control** is also needed, as each department has a limited budget. Our public representatives in office must provide **leadership** to the communities they serve. Government ministers must **motivate** staff in their departments. Good **communication** skills are needed to inform the public of government plans.

3.2: MANAGERS AND MANAGEMENT SKILLS

CHARACTERISTICS OF MANAGERS

- **Adaptable/flexible:** The business world is constantly changing, with new tastes, fashions, laws and technological developments. Managers must be able to adapt to these changes.
- **Competitive:** Business is very competitive and often involves the survival of the fittest. As a result, managers need to have a competitive nature.
- **Decisive:** Managers have to be able to make decisions quickly and also make tough decisions that may not always be popular.
- **Hard-working:** Hard work is necessary, as the manager may have to work long hours. Also, by working hard, the manager sets an example.
- **Human relations:** Managers need to be 'people persons'. They need to be good communicators since a large part of a manager's job involves communicating.
- **Organisation:** A good manager will make sure the firm is properly organised and has the right staff for each department.

- **Planning:** The manager needs to draw up long- and short-term plans for the business. A business with no plans is sure to fail.
- **Self-confident:** Managers need to have confidence in their own ability. There will be many challenges facing the business, and the manager must steer the firm through these.
- **Time management:** A certain amount of time should be given to each task. This may mean prioritising the more important tasks and perhaps delegating other tasks to other staff members.

> **Exam Tip:** It is unlikely that any more than **five** of these characteristics will be required. You can pick the ones that you find easiest to remember.

DIFFERENCES BETWEEN ENTERPRISE AND MANAGEMENT

- **Risk-taking:** Entrepreneurs are the people who take the financial risks of setting up the business. They stand to lose their money if the business is not a success. Managers, on the other hand, do not risk their own money.
- **Initiative:** The entrepreneur shows the initiative in coming up with the idea for the business. He/she spots the opportunity and goes for it. The manager, however, shows a different kind of initiative in solving day-to-day problems.
- **Day-to-day involvement:** The entrepreneur may not have the patience to work in the business on a daily basis. Thus, a manager is hired to do the day-to-day running of the business. The entrepreneur comes up with the idea and the manager puts those ideas into action.

MANAGEMENT SKILLS

Leadership

Leadership is a method of directing and influencing groups of people towards achieving objectives.

There are three main styles of leadership: **autocratic, democratic** and **laissez-faire**.

Autocratic

This is also known as authoritarian leadership.
- The manager does not consult with the staff.
- Staff are not trusted and are not allowed to use their initiative. This type of manager does not delegate.
- The autocratic manager does not like to be questioned.

As a result:

- Staff are usually resentful of this type of leadership. Industrial relations problems may result.
- Morale and motivation will be poor. This may cause absenteeism and labour turnover.
- By not listening to the opinions of staff, managers may lose a valuable source of good ideas for the firm.

Democratic

- Staff are consulted for their opinions.
- The manager has trust in the staff and allows them to use their initiative. Tasks are delegated to staff members.
- This manager encourages the workers and praises them for work done.

As a result:

- Morale is high in the workplace, as workers will feel that they are an important part of the organisation.
- By using their initiative, the staff can become a valuable source of ideas. Some employees will become intrapreneurs.
- The industrial relations climate in the firm will be good.

Laissez-faire

Also known as free rein or spectator management.

- Workers are left to get on with their jobs.
- A lot of trust and responsibility are placed in the staff.
- This style of management can result in intrapreneurship.

However:

- Depends on having highly responsible and motivated workers.
- Some workers become lazy and disinterested.

DIRECTION

- Directing involves getting people to do the jobs assigned to them.
- Direction requires good communication between the management and workers.

DELEGATION

Delegation involves giving staff members responsibility to do certain tasks and the authority to carry out those tasks.

- Management time is freed up to work on management issues.
- Work is often completed faster and more efficiently since the burden is shared.
- Staff morale is improved, as they feel more involved in the running of the business.
- Staff members develop leadership skills and some of them will become candidates for promotion in the future.

MOTIVATION

Motivation is the set of factors that cause people to act or behave in certain ways. Motivators may be financial or non-financial.

McGregor's Theory: Theory X and Theory Y

TABLE 3.2: MCGREGOR'S THEORY OF MOTIVATION

THEORY X WORKERS	THEORY Y WORKERS
• Dislike work and are lazy. • Will avoid responsibility. • Only want safety and security. • Do not care about the organisation or its goals. • Do not like and will resist change.	• Like work and are willing to work. • Like taking responsibility. • Want their esteem and self-actualisation needs met. • Care about the organisation and its goals. • Do not mind change and will accept it as normal.
THEORY X MANAGERS	THEORY Y MANAGERS
• Closely supervise and control the workers. • Do not delegate tasks to the workers. • Only rewards offered are financial ones. • Do not involve the staff in any decisions involving the business.	• Trust the workers to get on with their jobs. • Delegate jobs and responsibilities to staff. • Offer non-financial rewards like job enrichment, job satisfaction, etc. • Involve the staff in the decision-making.

Maslow's hierarchy of needs

Maslow stated that humans have five needs in ascending order. As one need is satisfied, the next one above it becomes the motivator. He arranged these in a hierarchy. As the needs at the bottom are satisfied, the individual is motivated to satisfy higher needs.

FIGURE 3.1: MASLOW'S HIERARCHY OF NEEDS

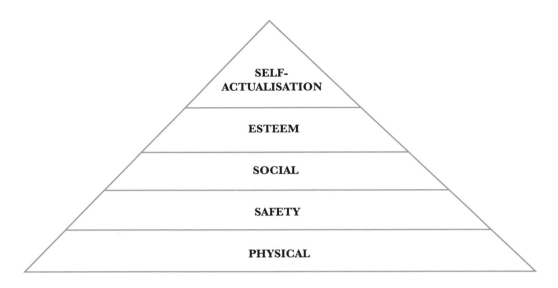

TABLE 3.3: APPLICATION OF MASLOW'S HIERARCHY TO THE WORKPLACE

NEED	SATISFIED BY
Self-actualisation needs	Delegating responsibility to staff, empowerment, share options and profit-sharing schemes. Opportunities for promotion.
Esteem needs	Promotion in the job, job title, size of office, praise and recognition, perks and rewards in the job.
Social needs	Good work atmosphere, social clubs, allowing social groupings to work together, staff outings.
Safety and security needs	Job security, membership of a trade union, contract of employment, industrial relations legislation.
Physiological needs	Proper conditions in the workplace, adequate wages, bonuses.

COMMUNICATION

Communication is the transfer of information between parties. This can be done orally, in writing or visually.

Importance of good communication in business

- **Employees:** Good communication with employees will lead to a good industrial relations climate and fewer problems.
- **Suppliers:** Raw materials will be delivered on time and payment will take place on time, which may result in discounts.
- **Customers:** Communication with customers will involve the firm advertising its goods or services. If this is done well, then the firm's sales and profits will grow.
- **Local community/public:** To achieve a good public image, a firm needs to keep in touch with the local community, e.g. sponsor a local event.
- **Shareholders:** Many firms depend on shareholders for their capital. As a result, they must be kept up to date on financial matters in the company.
- **Interest groups:** These can create a lot of bad publicity for a firm, so regular communication should be maintained with them.

Types of communication

- **Internal:** Communication that takes place within a business. There are different **channels of communication:**
  - ➤ **Downward:** Information that flows from management down to staff, e.g. instructions, orders, reports on performance.
  - ➤ **Upward:** This flows from staff up to management, e.g. requests for better pay and conditions, reporting back to managers.
  - ➤ **Horizontal:** People at the same level in the organisation exchange information, e.g. different department managers.
- **External:** Communication takes place between the business and outside stakeholders, e.g. suppliers, customers, other businesses, service providers, investors/banks, government, interest groups.

TABLE 3.4: METHODS OF COMMUNICATION

TYPE OF COMMUNICATION	VERBAL	WRITTEN	VISUAL/ELECTRONIC
Internal	Telephone, face-to-face conversation, intercom, meetings.	Reports, memos, notice boards, letters, newsletters.	Graphs and charts, data projector, video.
External	Telephone, meetings, TV and radio, exhibitions and trade fairs, press releases.	Business letters, reports, newspapers, brochures, e-mail, publicity post.	Video conferencing, e-mail, electronic data interchange (EDI), website.

Principles of good communication/factors that ensure managers communicate effectively

- **Proper language:** Managers should ensure that they use language that can be understood by staff and avoid technical terms.
- **Brief/concise:** A message should be short and to the point. If a message contains too much information, the real meaning of the message may be lost.
- **Correct timing:** The message should be delivered at the correct time. An important staff announcement should be made on a Monday morning, not on a Friday evening.
- **Allow feedback:** The sender should get feedback from the audience to make sure the message has been received and understood.
- **Record:** A record should be kept of the communication so that if there are any issues arising from it, the parties can check what was agreed.
- **Good relationship:** If a good relationship exists between the sender and receiver, then there is a better chance of decisions being agreed upon.
- **Suitable method:** The correct medium should be used, e.g. an employee getting a warning about their conduct should get it in a private manner and not in public.

Exam Tip: State the principle and then say how/why it is important.

Barriers to effective communications

- **Wrong language:** If the manager uses too much technical language, the recipient may not understand the message.
- **Padding:** This means including too much information. The real message may end up getting lost or the receiver may lose patience.
- **Wrong timing:** If the timing of the message is wrong then it may be lost, e.g. an important announcement on Friday afternoon may not be properly received.
- **Lack of feedback:** If the person giving the message does not get feedback, he/she will not know if the message has been delivered properly.
- **No record:** If no record is kept of what was agreed, then disputes might arise in the future.
- **Poor relationship:** If a poor relationship exists between the sender and receiver, then the receiver may not believe what the sender is saying, even if it is true.
- **Wrong method or medium:** The communication will be ineffective if the wrong method or medium is used, e.g. an important announcement over the intercom where a meeting may be necessary.

Exam Tip: State the barrier and then say how/why it is a barrier. Note that if the principles of effective communications are reversed, this means the barriers.

Factors to be considered when choosing the most effective method of communication

- **Cost:** Some methods are more expensive than others, e.g. an international phone call is dearer than sending an e-mail.
- **Urgency:** If a message is urgently required, then certain methods are better, e.g. a phone call is quicker than a business letter.
- **Confidentiality:** If the message is of a confidential nature, a face-to-face meeting is best, e.g. a worker being laid off.
- **Record:** If a record of the message is needed, a written communication will be best.
- **Feedback:** If the sender of the message wants feedback, a method should be chosen that allows this, e.g. a meeting.
- **Nature of the message:** If the message is detailed and complicated, a written format is best, as it can be read and studied.
- **Legal requirements:** Some business communications, e.g. contracts, must be in written form. Therefore, they have to be sent in print form in the post.

Exam Tip: State the factor and then say how/why it is a factor.

MEETINGS

- **Ad hoc meeting:** A meeting that takes place at short notice to discuss a matter that has arisen unexpectedly.
- **Annual general meeting (AGM):** The main meeting of the shareholders of a company (or club) once a year.
- **Extraordinary general meeting (EGM):** A meeting called by the company to discuss an urgent matter that cannot wait until the AGM, e.g. a legal claim against the company.

Duties/role of the chairperson

In relation to meetings, the chairperson should:
- Set the agenda in consultation with the secretary.
- Open the meeting and ensure that a quorum is present. (A quorum is the minimum number of people that must be present.)
- Have the minutes of the previous meeting read and adopted by those present. The chairperson then signs the minutes.
- Make sure the meeting runs in an orderly manner and the agenda is followed.
- Allow everyone a chance to speak and participate in the meeting.
- Put motions to a vote. In the event of a tie, the chairperson has the casting (deciding) vote.

Duties/role of the secretary

- Set the agenda for the meeting in consultation with the chairperson.
- Send out the notice and agenda of the meeting to all who are entitled to attend.
- Read the minutes of the previous meeting.
- Read any correspondence received by the company/club.
- Take written notes at the meeting and write up the minutes.
- Arrange the next meeting.

> **Exam Tip:** It should be sufficient to know **five** duties of a chairperson and secretary.

Notice and agenda

A notice and an agenda of all meetings must be sent out by the secretary to all those eligible to attend. Below are a sample notice, agenda and minutes for a **limited company**.

TABLE 3.5: NOTICE AND AGENDA OF A COMPANY

NOTICE AND AGENDA FOR THE AGM OF CREATIVE SOLUTIONS LTD

Notice is hereby given that the fifth AGM of Creative Solutions Ltd will be held at the company's office in Grange St, Dublin 6, on 16 February 2008 at 2:00 p.m. for the following purposes:

1. Minutes of the 2007 AGM.
2. Matters arising from the minutes.
3. Chairperson's report.
4. Auditor's report.
5. Proposed dividends for the year.
6. Election of directors.
7. Appointment of auditors.
8. Auditor's fees.
9. Any other business.

By order of the board,

D. McCabe
D. McCabe
Company secretary

Minutes of a meeting

The minutes are written up after the meeting.

TABLE 3.6: MINUTES OF THE AGM OF A LIMITED COMPANY

MINUTES OF THE AGM OF CREATIVE SOLUTIONS LTD

The fifth annual general meeting of Creative Solutions Ltd was held in the company's office in Grange St, Dublin 6, on 16 February 2008.

    The chairperson, secretary, auditor and 20 shareholders were present.

1. The minutes of the 2007 AGM were read, adopted and signed by the chairperson, Bob Breen.
2. There were no matters arising from the minutes.
3. The chairperson, Bob Breen, gave his report. He announced his satisfaction with the company performance in 2007 and outlined plans for the expansion programme in 2008.
4. The auditor, Paul Dunne, presented his report and this was approved unanimously.
5. A dividend of 6 per cent was declared.
6. G. Cohen, N. Stiles and M. Peters were re-elected as directors.
7. S. Crozier and Company were reappointed as company auditors.
8. A 10 per cent increase in the auditor's fee from 2007 was approved.
9. There being no other business, the meeting closed at 5:00 p.m.

Bob Breen
Bob Breen, Chairperson
19 February 2008

Exam Tip: It should be sufficient to know **five** points of an agenda and **five** points for the minutes. If asked to write an agenda and minutes, the minutes should correspond to the points chosen for the agenda.

The following is a sample notice, agenda and minutes for a **club**.

TABLE 3.7: NOTICE AND AGENDA FOR A CLUB

NOTICE AND AGENDA FOR THE RINGSIDE BOXING CLUB

Notice is hereby given that the 8th AGM of the Ringside Boxing Club will be held in the clubhouse in Cavan Town on 10 March 2008 at 8:00 p.m. The following will be the agenda:

1. Minutes of the 2007 AGM.
2. Matters arising from the minutes.
3. Correspondence.
4. Chairperson's report.
5. Treasurer's report.
6. Election of officers for the year ahead.
7. Sponsorship.
8. AOB.

Liam Burke
Liam Burke
Club secretary

TABLE 3.8: MINUTES OF THE AGM OF A CLUB

MINUTES OF THE AGM OF RINGSIDE BOXING CLUB

The 8th AGM of the Ringside Boxing Club was held in the clubhouse in Cavan Town on 10 March 2008. The chairperson, Andrew Murray, and 16 members attended.

1. The minutes of the previous AGM were read, adopted and signed by the chairperson, Andrew Murray.
2. There were no matters arising from the minutes.
3. A letter was read from the Liverpool Boxing Club thanking Cavan Boxing Club for their hospitality on their visit.
4. The chairperson gave his report on the year's activities.
5. The treasurer, A. McDermott, presented his report. The accounts showed a surplus for the year of €7000.
6. The outgoing officers were re-elected unanimously.
7. A new sponsor, G. McTaggart, promised €2000 to sponsor the tournament.
8. There being no other business, the chairperson closed the meeting.

Andrew Murray
Andrew Murray
Chairperson

WRITTEN COMMUNICATIONS IN BUSINESS

The main types of written communications in business are **memos**, **business letters** and **reports**.

The following is a sample memo to department managers outlining two methods of expansion that will be discussed at an upcoming meeting.

TABLE 3.9: MEMO

MEMO

TO: All department managers
FROM: Kevin Dillon, managing director
DATE: 6 April 2008
RE: In our manager's meeting on 21 April, we will be discussing methods of expanding the business. This will involve a discussion on mergers and alliances.

Signed: *Kevin Dillon*
Managing Director

The following is a sample business letter to the managing director of a firm outlining possible barriers to effective communications.

TABLE 3.10: BUSINESS LETTER

LACEY CONSULTANTS
Abbeyside Park, Waterford City
Phone (052) 223344. E-mail laceycon@eircom.net

19 June 2008

Creative Solutions Ltd
Grange St
Dublin 6

Re: Barriers to effective communications

Dear Mr Breen,

We have identified the following barriers to effective communications:

1. Wrong language: Your managers need to use simple and easy-to-understand language and not technical jargon.
2. Padding: Sometimes your managers use too much information, which clouds the real meaning of the message.
3. Wrong timing: Some information has been communicated to staff at the end of the working day. They are not really tuned in at this time and just want to go home.
4. Lack of feedback: Your staff are often not given a chance to respond to information given to them.

Hopefully these findings can be of assistance to your firm.

Yours sincerely,
Des Lacey
Des Lacey
Managing Director

The following is a sample report to the managing director of a financial services company outlining the benefits of a human resource department to the company.

TABLE 3.11: BUSINESS REPORT

REPORT ON BENEFITS OF A HUMAN RESOURCE DEPARTMENT TO STAR FINANCIAL SERVICES LTD

To: Star Financial Services Ltd

From: Lacey Consultants

Date: 12 July 2008

Terms of reference: Benefits of introducing a human resource department to Star Financial Services Ltd.

Findings: A HR department will bring the following benefits:

1. Recruitment and selection: The HR department will specialise in recruiting and selecting staff. Job descriptions and person specifications will be prepared and interviews will be carried out.
2. Training and development: Induction training will be offered to new staff. Further on-the-job and off-the-job training will be given as needed to upgrade skills.
3. Performance appraisal: The HR manager will assess the performance of staff members. Goals can be set and suitable candidates can be chosen for promotion.
4. Reward: A rewards system can be put in place. This may involve financial rewards such as bonuses, commissions and profit sharing. Non-financial rewards may include job enrichment, flexitime and social events.
5. Employer/employee relations: A HR department will work towards maintaining good industrial relations.

Recommendations: Since this firm has grown for the past five years, it is now recommended that a human resource department be set up in the company.

Des Lacey

Des Lacey
Managing Director, Lacey Consultants

Exam Tip: If asked to do a letter or a report on a given topic, the **layout** of the letter/report will contribute towards the **smaller** portion of the marks. The information sought will count for a significantly greater portion of the marks. For example, a report question for 20 marks might have a marking scheme of 4–6 marks for the report layout and the remaining 14–16 marks for the information.

Information and communications technology (ICT)

The following are some of the applications of IT in business communications.

- **Spreadsheets:** Software packages that firms use to do accounting and numerical work, e.g. budgeting forecasts, costing estimates.
- **Electronic data interchange (EDI):** Orders can be sent automatically from a buyer's computer to a supplier's computer when stock levels fall to a certain point.
- **Video conferencing:** A 'virtual' meeting held between people who are in different locations using computer or television screens. These meetings save a firm time and money as no travelling need take place.
- **Internet:** A worldwide network of millions of computers connected together. Information is transferred quickly and cheaply via e-mail to other firms' computer systems. A major use of the internet for business is the World Wide Web (WWW). Most companies have their own website where they advertise their goods.
- **Electronic mail (e-mail):** This is a means of communicating quickly and cheaply over the internet. It is popular with both business and individual users. However, an increasing problem with the internet and e-mail is viruses.
- **E-business:** When companies do some of their business online, i.e. transact business over the internet, both with other companies and with consumers. Consumers can log on to a company's website and make a purchase with a credit card. One of the main problems of online business is the danger of credit card fraud.

Advantages of ICT

- Huge amounts of data can be received and processed quickly. This improves the quality of decision making in the firm.
- Businesses can now advertise and promote their goods and services online through their websites.
- Many firms now sell their goods and services over the internet.
- Businesses can save time and money by using video conferencing, which removes the need for travelling to meetings.
- Some staff may be able to work from home. This makes geographic location less important and may allow firms to work from smaller premises.
- Dealings with suppliers are more efficient through the EDI system. Stocks are automatically reordered when they fall to certain levels.

Disadvantages of ICT

- The initial installation costs are high. Due to advances in technology, systems must be upgraded on a regular basis.
- Staff have to be trained to use the new technology. This can be costly and cause disruption to the business.

- An increasing problem with the use of the internet in business is viruses.
- When firms do business online, there is a danger of credit card fraud. As a result, some consumers will not do business over the internet.
- Sometimes there are problems of security with important information. Hackers may gain access to important files.
- Companies regularly receive large amounts of junk mail (spam), which can clog up the system and take time to clear off.

EXAM QUESTIONS

Exam question 1

Draft a memo. (10 marks)

Marking scheme

This question tends to come up in the short questions. The marking schemes have tended to be **six points** at **1 mark** each for the layout of the memo (heading, to, from, date, re, signed) and **4 marks** for two pieces of information. See the sample memo on p. 33.

Exam question 2

Illustrate what is meant by 'terms of reference'. (10 marks)

Marking scheme

Two pieces of information are needed, probably at **5 marks** each.

Sample answer

The terms of reference is one of the headings of a report. **(5 marks)** It outlines the subject matter of the report, i.e. what the report was written about. **(5 marks)**

Exam question 3

On average, managers spend over 75 per cent of their time communicating. Explain the factors that ensure managers communicate effectively. Use examples where appropriate. (25 marks)

Marking scheme

Five factors are required at **5 marks** each. The 5 marks is split into **2 marks** for naming the factor and **3 marks** for developing the point. It would be possible to get full marks without an example.

Sample answer

- **Appropriate language (2 marks):** The communication will be effective if the sender uses a language that the receiver understands, i.e. avoids technical terms. **(3 marks)**
- **Brief and to the point (2 marks):** If the manager gets straight to the point, then the staff and other stakeholders will understand the communication. A long-winded message only loses its audience as people lose patience. **(3 marks)**
- **Proper planning/being prepared (2 marks):** The message should be structured and properly prepared by the sender. For example, a manager delivering a sales report should know the background to the report. **(3 marks)**
- **Allow feedback (2 marks):** The manager should allow and indeed seek feedback from the receiver of the communication. By doing this, both parties are sure that they understand each other. **(3 marks)**
- **Correct method/medium (2 marks):** The medium most appropriate to the situation should be used. For example, if the manager is explaining a complex matter, then charts and diagrams could be used to support and summarise the main information. **(3 marks)**

3.3: MANAGEMENT ACTIVITIES

PLANNING

Planning means setting objectives and deciding on the methods to be used to achieve these objectives.

Principles of planning

All plans must follow the SMART principles. Plans should be:
- **Specific:** Plans must clearly state what they are trying to achieve.
- **Measurable:** It should be possible to measure the success of the plan.
- **Agreed:** Plans should be agreed upon by all the staff before being implemented.
- **Realistic:** Managers must be realistic when setting targets and ensure that they are achievable.
- **Timing:** Any plan should be capable of being achieved within a reasonable timeframe. Otherwise the plan will just fizzle out.

SWOT analysis

- **Strengths:** Strengths may include a highly skilled workforce, a good industrial relations climate and a strong cash flow position.
- **Weaknesses:** All businesses have some weaknesses. Perhaps the firm gives too much credit, is weak on training its staff or has outdated IT facilities.
- **Opportunities:** Examples of opportunities might include getting into new markets, developing new products or cutting costs by using more efficient production methods.
- **Threats:** Threats may include new competitors coming into the market, rising labour costs or keeping up with rapid developments in IT.

Types of plans

- **Grand strategic plan (mission statement):** The mission statement outlines the entire purpose of the organisation. In a way it is the philosophy of the company. For example, Superquinn's mission statement is 'to be a world-class team renowned for excellence in fresh food and customer service'.
- **Strategic plans:** These are long-term plans that may have a timeframe of up to five years. They are drawn up by the board of directors. They set long-term objectives for the firm, e.g. a plan to open five new branches in the next five years.
- **Tactical plans:** These are short- to medium-term plans, e.g. one to two years. Senior and middle management will be involved in drawing them up. An example of a tactical plan is a three-month advertising campaign to try to boost sales by 10 per cent.
- **Operational plans:** Short-term plans that involve targets for the weeks and months ahead, e.g. monthly budgets and cash flow statements. Middle management may draw them up.
- **Contingency plans:** Plans to deal with specific problems that might arise. They will outline procedures to follow, e.g. what to do in the event of a fire in the firm.

Benefits of planning

- Planning helps to **remove uncertainty**. If a firm has planned for the future, then it should be able to cope with change.
- By planning ahead, the firm will be able to **anticipate problems**.
- Plans give a firm a **focus and direction**. Without plans, any firm will drift aimlessly.
- Having plans serves to **motivate** staff and management in the company. Plans involve setting targets and staff will be motivated to try to achieve these targets.
- Plans provide a **benchmark** against which actual performance can be compared to targets that have been set.
- The business will need to present plans to the **bank** if it is **seeking finance**. These plans will include a business plan and cash flow forecasts.

ORGANISING

Organisation charts are diagrams that show the management structure in an organisation.

Functional/line structure

This type of structure divides the business into its various departments/functions.

FIGURE 3.2: FUNCTIONAL STRUCTURE

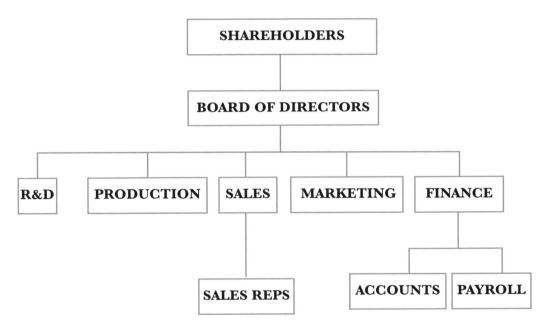

Advantages:
- Everyone knows their position in the firm and who they are answerable to.
- This structure provides scope for promotion, which is a motivational tool for workers.

Disadvantages:
- Departments may become little worlds of their own where employees may focus on departmental rather than organisational goals.
- Communication and co-ordination between functional departments may not be good, which may lead to slow decision-making.

Span of control

The span of control relates to the number of subordinates who report to one supervisor or manager.

A **wide span of control** is where a manager has control over a large number of subordinates.

A **narrow span of control** is where a manager has only a small number of subordinates answerable to him or her.

FIGURE 3.3: SPAN OF CONTROL

- With a narrow span of control, more attention can be given to each staff member, and each worker has easier access to his/her boss.
- The span of control depends on the type of work, the quality of the workers and the resources of the firm.

Line and staff

Line and staff organisation is where the line structure is applied as usual, together with specialist functions to assist all departments, e.g. a HR department or an IT department.

FIGURE 3.4: LINE AND STAFF

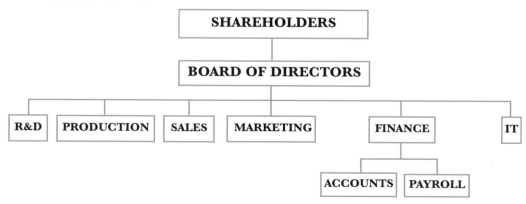

Here the IT function is a service function whose role is to serve the other departments.

Delayering involves the removal of some of the layers of middle management from the management structure in order to cut costs and improve communications.

Matrix structure

The matrix structure is where employees are organised into **teams**. Teams may be formed to complete a project, such as developing a new product.

FIGURE 3.5: MATRIX STRUCTURE

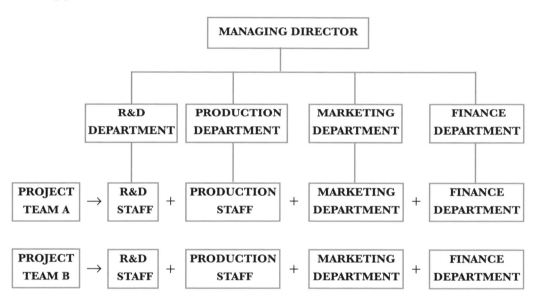

Advantages:
- The strengths of the various departments are combined.
- There is higher staff morale since every department is involved.
- Efficiency is improved. Because departments are working together, there will be no duplication of work.

Disadvantages:
- Good communication and interpersonal skills are needed.
- Decision making may be slowed down.
- Power struggles may result as individuals seek to take control of the project and get all the credit.

The matrix structure is very similar to a **project team**. Projects may last for months or even years.

Product structure

Sometimes organisations may have very different product lines. In such a case each product would have its own departments.

Below is the management structure of a financial institution.

FIGURE 3.6: PRODUCT STRUCTURE

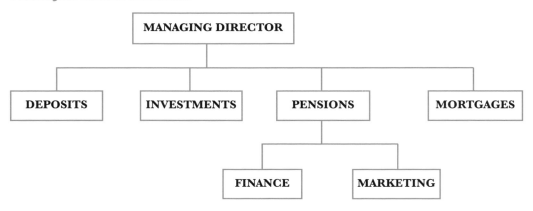

Geographic structure

A business may be organised according to the geographical market it serves. The business is regionalised, with a different manager in each region.

FIGURE 3.7: GEOGRAPHIC STRUCTURE

CONTROLLING

Controlling involves monitoring performance, comparing it to the targets set and taking corrective action where required.

There are three types of control: stock control, credit control and quality control.

Stock control

Stock control involves having the right quantity of stock on hand to meet customer demand, while at the same time not holding too much and incurring costs.

The correct amount of stock is called the **optimum level**.

TABLE 3.12: OPTIMUM STOCK

TOO MUCH STOCK	TOO LITTLE STOCK
• Cash is tied up. • Risk of going out of date/ obsolescence. • Storage and insurance costs.	• Risk of stock-outs and loss of sales as a result. • Loss of profits due to loss of sales. • Loss of customer confidence.

Buffer stock is the minimum level of stock that should be held. Stocks should not be allowed to fall below this level. Once levels fall to this amount, more stock should be ordered.

Just-in-time (JIT)

This is a stock control system developed by the Japanese to minimise the costs of holding stocks of raw materials, work in progress and finished goods.

JIT means making goods to order just before they are required. Deliveries of raw materials arrive just in time for them to be used in the production process. This cuts down on storage and holding costs. It is a means of cutting costs and gaining a competitive edge. However, in order to work properly, a very efficient ordering system and very reliable delivery system are needed. Firms should ensure that they have a good **stock control system** in place. Good stock control involves regular stock-taking.

Credit control

Credit control involves deciding which customers are given credit, how much they are given and ensuring that they pay on time.

Granting credit costs firms money. There are costs such as money tied up and loss of possible interest, administrative costs involved in keeping records of the debtors and possible bad debts.

When firms sell on credit, they create **debtors.** These debtors need to be controlled. This is the job of the **credit control department**. Most large businesses will have such a department.

Role of credit controller:
- Decide whether or not credit should be given.
- Investigate the customer's creditworthiness. The best way to do this is to get a trade reference from others who have dealt with the customer.
- Decide the credit limit to give the customer and agree the credit period.
- Encourage debtors to pay on time. This can be achieved by offering discounts for prompt payment.
- Review the credit limits of existing customers at regular intervals. Limits may be extended or reduced.

A **bad debt** is when a debtor fails to pay some or all of what they owe. Bad debts can be **reduced** in the following ways:
- Do not sell on credit to any customers who have poor credit histories.
- Have a good credit control department that involves invoices being sent out on time and regular reminders for late payers.
- Offer financial incentives to debtors to pay on time, e.g. discounts.
- Employ the services of a debt collection agency to collect the money if necessary.
- Take out insurance against bad debts.

Quality control

Quality control is the process of checking the standard of goods and services produced by a business to ensure that they are of a high quality.

Q Mark
This is an award of quality given to Irish businesses by Excellence Ireland if they achieve high standards. This is of great benefit to the firm, as customers recognise its quality.
- Shows that the firm has high standards of quality control.
- Gives the firm a marketing advantage.
- Used as a stepping-stone to ISO 9002 series.

International Quality Standards – ISO 9002 Series
The International Standards Organisation (ISO) has introduced a set of standards which show that a firm has quality production processes and makes a quality product.

Advantages of ISO 9002:

- It is a very valuable marketing and exporting tool. Firms that have the symbol have an advantage in the marketplace.
- It shows that the firm has undergone an independent inspection.
- It motivates employees by recognising their contribution to the quality ethos in the firm.
- It enables the firm to tender for government contracts, which are only given to firms with ISO 9002.
- Firms that do not have the ISO 9002 will not qualify for certain government grants and may have difficulty getting bank loans.

Quality circles

This is a group of workers who meet voluntarily and regularly to identify and solve problems in relation to their work. They try to find solutions to problems that meet with management approval. Management has an important role to play, as time and money need to be allocated to allow the circles to operate. Managers must also be prepared to meet with the groups.

Quality control

Quality control involves checking for errors during and after the production process. It also means checking raw materials for defects before production begins. Co-operation is needed between the stock control manager, production manager and quality control department. The emphasis is on getting it right the first time.

EXAM QUESTIONS

Exam question 1

Draft and label a typical organisational structure for an organisation of your choice. (10 marks)

Marking scheme

This question has appeared in the short questions on numerous occasions. A labelled diagram of a functional or matrix structure would get full marks.

Exam question 2

Planning/organising/controlling is the most important management activity. (a) Do you agree with this statement? (b) Explain why mangers would deem this to be true. (20 marks)

Marking scheme

If you are asked whether you agree or not, then you can choose to disagree and pick one of the other two activities. If you agree, then talk about the activity given. Do not do a combination of both.

Exam question 3

Evaluate how two different types of planning contribute to the success of a business or community enterprise. Use examples in your answer. (20 marks)

Marking scheme

The scheme is based on **two** types of planning at **10 marks** each – **2 marks** for a name of a type of plan, **4 marks** for a piece of information on it and **4 marks** for an example of it in business or the community.

Sample answer

- **Tactical planning (2 marks):** Tactical plans are short- to medium-term plans of one or two years. They are sometimes called operational plans. Plans of any kind give a firm a focus and direction. **(4 marks)** Examples of tactical planning in a business are strategies to attract customers, devising training programs for staff or organising stock and quality control systems. **(4 marks)**
- **Strategic planning (2 marks):** These are the firm's long-term plans. They may be set for up to five years in the future. Strategic planning usually involves doing a SWOT analysis, where the firm looks at its strengths, weaknesses, opportunities and threats. **(4 marks)** Examples of strategic planning in a firm are trying to increase market share, opening new branches and strategies to reduce debt. **(4 marks)**

IMPORTANT DEFINITIONS FROM UNIT 3

- **Leadership:** Leadership is a method of directing and influencing groups of people towards achieving objectives.
- **Delegation:** Delegation involves giving staff members responsibility to do certain tasks and the authority to carry out those tasks.
- **Motivation:** The set of factors that cause people to act or behave in certain ways. These motivators may be financial or non-financial.
- **Communication:** The transfer of information between parties. Communication can be verbal, written or visual/electronic. Communication can be upward, downward or horizontal.
- **Agenda:** A list of topics to be discussed at a meeting in the order in which they are to be discussed. The chairperson ensures that the agenda is followed.
- **Minutes:** A written record of what was discussed at a meeting. They contain details of decisions made and are read out at the next meeting.
- **Quorum:** The minimum number of people that must be present for a meeting to take place. The quorum is listed in the company's articles of association.
- **Standing order:** Rules that govern how a meeting should be run. The chairperson makes sure they are followed.
- **Terms of reference:** The reason for the report being written. It is one of the headings of the report.
- **Video conferencing:** This is when a meeting takes place with people in different locations using computer or television screens. It is often called a virtual meeting and can save a company time and money.
- **Internet:** A worldwide network of millions of computers connected together through phone lines, broadband cables, etc. Information is rapidly transferred between geographic locations.
- **Electronic data interchange (EDI):** A computer-to-computer exchange of data between businesses. For example, goods can be ordered and invoices can be sent online.
- **E-business (electronic business):** Business transacted over the internet. Businesses can buy, sell and promote their goods online, while consumers can buy a wide range of goods and services and pay by credit card over the internet.
- **Spreadsheets:** Software packages that firms use to do accounting and numerical work. Budgeting, cash flows, accounting data, costing analyses, etc. can be presented on spreadsheets.
- **Planning:** Planning involves setting goals for an organisation and developing strategies by which they can be achieved.
- **SWOT analysis:** An assessment that a firm makes of its internal strengths and weaknesses and external opportunities and threats.

- **Chain of command:** The people through whom information flows as it goes from the top of the organisation to the bottom.
- **Span of control:** The number of subordinates reporting to one supervisor or manager. A span of control can be wide or narrow.
- **Delayering:** This involves reducing the layers/tiers of management in an organisation. The purpose of delayering is usually to cut costs.
- **Stock control:** Monitoring the stock levels in a business to make sure the right quantity is kept to meet customer demand while at the same time not holding too much and incurring costs.
- **Just-in-time:** A system of stock control whereby a firm keeps stock levels of both raw materials and finished goods at a minimum in order to cut costs. Raw materials are delivered as they are needed for production.
- **Credit control:** This involves controlling the timing and amount of credit given to customers. The purpose of credit control is to ensure the firm gets paid on time and bad debts are kept to a minimum.
- **Quality control:** The process of checking the standard of goods and services produced by a firm to ensure that they are of high quality. Faulty goods/services are removed.

CHAPTER 4
Unit 4: Managing II

4.1: HOUSEHOLD AND BUSINESS MANAGER

This unit compares **households** and **businesses** under the headings of **finance, insurance** and **taxation**.

FINANCE

Finance for a household or a business can be short term (up to one year), medium term (one to five years) or long term (five years and up).

TABLE 4.1: SOURCES OF FINANCE

SHORT TERM	EXPLANATION	ADVANTAGE	DISADVANTAGE
Bank overdraft	Permission from a bank to the account holder to withdraw more money than is in the account, up to an agreed limit.	Easy to obtain and no security is required.	Rate of interest is high – can be up to 12%.
Trade credit	When a firm buys stock on credit from its suppliers but does not pay for one to two months.	Happens naturally in business and no security is required.	Business may lose out on cash discounts. Late payment can lead to a damaged credit rating.
Accrued expenses	Firms get certain services supplied and pay in arrears, e.g. telephone, gas.	There is no cost involved and it is created naturally.	Amounts involved are small and services may be cut off for late payment.
Factoring debts	Selling debts to a factoring (finance) firm at a discount in return for immediate cash.	The firm gets what it is owed from its debtors immediately. Hassle of collecting is passed on.	The discount taken can be large, so it can be expensive.

TABLE 4.1: SOURCES OF FINANCE (CONTINUED)

MEDIUM TERM	EXPLANATION	ADVANTAGE	DISADVANTAGE
Term loan	A loan with fixed interest and principal repayments.	Interest payments are tax deductible for a business.	The bank often requires security.
Hire purchase	A finance company pays the seller and the buyer pays the finance company in instalments.	Have the use of the asset before owning it. Interest payments are tax deductible.	Can be an expensive form of financing.
Leasing	A finance company pays the seller and the buyer pays the finance company the rental payments.	Use of modern assets without buying. Can upgrade. No security needed.	Never own the asset.
LONG TERM	EXPLANATION	ADVANTAGE	DISADVANTAGE
Share capital	The firm sells shares (part-ownership) in the business. Shareholders get a share of the profits, called a dividend.	Does not have to be repaid. Interest-free finance.	Loss of control by the original owners.
Retained earnings	Past profits of the business that have been retained for future development.	A free source of finance since it does not have to be repaid.	Shareholders may be unhappy if too much is retained and not paid as dividends.
Long-term loan	A loan of over five years secured on the fixed assets of the business. Also called debentures.	Interest payments are tax deductible. No control of the company is lost.	Security is required. Long-term loans increase the financial risk (gearing) of the business.
Grants	Non-repayable amounts given by the government and/or the EU to Irish businesses.	They do not have to be repaid.	The firm may have to create a certain number of jobs.

Exam Tip: You should know **three** examples of each source of finance.

Factors to consider when choosing a source of finance

- **Purpose of finance:** If the finance is needed for a long-term purpose, e.g. purchase of fixed assets, then a long-term source should be used, e.g. long-term loan.
- **Cost of finance:** In times of high interest rates, loans may be expensive. Selling shares may be a better option in this case.
- **Existing borrowings/gearing:** If a firm has a lot of existing loans, i.e. is highly geared, then getting a further loan may affect the company's ability to repay it.
- **Control:** Issuing/selling shares to raise finance involves a loss of control in the company, whereas getting loan finance does not.
- **Security required:** Banks will usually require security before giving loans. Issuing shares, on the other hand, does not require any security.
- **Tax implications:** Interest on loan capital is tax deductible, whereas dividends on share capital are not.

Factors taken into account by a bank before granting finance

- **Purpose and duration of the finance:** How much is required and for how long?
- **Existing borrowings:** Banks may be reluctant to lend to firms that already have a high level of debt, as the risk of not getting repaid is increased. This is called high gearing.
- **Security available:** A business must be able to offer security for all long-term loans and sometimes for medium-term loans as well.
- **Credit history:** The bank will check the firm's track record in repaying previous loans before granting any new/additional loan.
- **Ability to repay:** The business must provide evidence of ability to repay any finance. This will involve past profit and loss accounts and cash flow forecasts of expected future earnings.

Cash flow forecast

A cash flow forecast is an estimate of the expected future inflows to and out-flows from a business (or household) for a period of time into the future.

Advantages of cash flow forecasts
- A cash flow is an important **planning tool** for any business, as it shows expected future inflows and outflows.
- The forecast will highlight periods when the firm may have **shortages**. Finance can be organised to deal with the shortage.
- They identify times of **surpluses**. Uses can then be found for this extra finance.
- They are essential if the firm is looking for **finance** from a bank, as they show if the firm is able to repay loans.

TABLE 4.2: SAMPLE CASH FLOW FORECAST

	JAN	FEB	MAR	APR	TOTAL
Total income	80,000	90,000	95,000	105,000	370,000
Total expenditure	85,000	80,000	105,000	80,000	350,000
Net cash	(5,000)	10,000	(10,000)	25,000	20,000
Opening cash	**3,000**	(2,000)	8,000	(2,000)	3,000
Closing cash	(2,000)	8,000	(2,000)	23,000	**23,000**

1. In which months is the firm experiencing cash flow problems?

January and March (the months with negative net cash figures).

2. Explain possible reasons for the problems.

Not controlling expenses properly, not getting paid by debtors on time, paying creditors more quickly than necessary, not spreading out expenses.

3. Suggest possible solutions to the problems.

Have proper control over expenses, improve credit control, which will result in debtors paying on time, delay payments to creditors, get short-term finance, e.g. bank overdraft. Overall, however, the outlook is positive, as the opening cash balance of €3,000 is increased to €23,000 closing cash at the end of the four months.

> **Exam Tip:** You will not be asked to prepare a cash flow forecast, but rather, to interpret and answer questions on one. The most important line in a cash flow forecast is the **net cash** line.

INSURANCE

Principles of insurance

- **Insurable interest:** An insured person must gain by something's existence and suffer financially by its loss, e.g. a business owner could insure the life of a key person in the business, but not the life of a family member.
- **Utmost good faith:** When filling in the proposal form, all material/important facts must be disclosed. A material fact is one that would influence the premium being charged, e.g. a business storing flammable materials in a shed beside the factory.
- **Indemnity:** The insured cannot make a profit from insurance. The insured should be placed in the same position financially after the accident as they were before the accident, e.g. if a property that was worth €600,000 was insured for €700,000 and was destroyed by a fire, then the insured will only receive €600,000 in compensation.

- **Subrogation:** Once the insurance company pays compensation to the insured, it then acquires any third party rights to try to recover any of the money it paid out, e.g. if a builder damages a property when building beside it, the insurance company will compensate the property owner, but can then sue the builder to try to recover its money.
- **Contribution:** If an insured party insures an item with two insurance companies, then he/she will still only get compensation to the value of the loss. The insurance company that pays the compensation will in turn be compensated in part by the other company.

Exam Tip: You should know **three** principles of insurance.

Average clause

The average clause states that if something is only insured for part of its value, then the compensation paid will be the same proportion of the damage as the proportion of its value for which it was insured. This prevents the insured from **underinsuring** assets.

For example, suppose premises valued at €1,000,000 were only insured for €800,000. A fire then caused €200,000 worth of damage. The compensation paid will be €160,000, i.e. four-fifths of the €200,000, the same fraction of its value for which it is insured.

Household insurances

- **Motor insurance:** This is compulsory by law. Motor insurance can be third party, third party fire and theft or comprehensive.
- **Buildings and contents insurance:** This covers against all risks.
- **Life assurance:** This provides for the next of kin in the event of the death of the principal in the family. Life assurance can be whole life or endowment.
- **Health insurance:** This covers the costs of medical treatment and hospital costs when family members get ill.
- **Mortgage protection insurance:** Banks and building societies insist on borrowers taking this out when they get a mortgage.
- **Pay Related Social Insurance (PRSI):** A compulsory deduction from a person's wages that goes towards unemployment benefits, maternity payment, sickness pay, etc.

Business insurances

- **Motor insurance:** Same as for the household.
- **Buildings and contents insurance:** Same as for household, but covers stock as well.
- **Consequential loss:** Covers the business against loss of earnings due to being closed as a result of a fire or other accident.

- **Employers' liability:** This covers the firm against claims made by employees who have accidents or are injured at work.
- **Public liability:** Covers the firm for claims made by members of the public who are injured while on the company's premises.
- **Product liability:** Protects the business in the event of claims made by customers who suffer loss or injury while using the firm's products.
- **Fidelity guarantee:** Insures the business against financial loss as a result of employees' dishonesty.
- **Goods and cash in transit:** Provides cover for loss as a result of goods or cash being transported.

Advantage of insurance to a business

- There may be a **legal requirement** for a business to take out certain insurances, e.g. motor insurance and PRSI.
- Insurance guarantees the **survival** and continuance of the business even in the event of an accident.
- Insurance protects the firm's **cash flow**. Large amounts do not have to be paid out of the firm's own resources.
- **Safety standards** are improved in the firm since insurance companies insist on certain precautions being taken before offering insurance cover, e.g. fire exits and smoke alarms.

Risk management

The greater the risk, the higher the premium. As a result, both households and businesses both try to reduce the risk involved in order to reduce the premium. Methods might include the following.

- Be security conscious and install security devices such as CCTV cameras, alarms, fire doors, etc.
- Provide training courses for the staff in health and safety issues.
- Firms can keep stock levels low, which will reduce the premium.

Insurance terms

- **Actuary:** The person who calculates the premium that the insured should pay. The actuary works for the insurance company.
- **Assessor:** The person who calculates the amount of compensation the insured gets in the event of a loss.
- **Loading:** An additional charge on the premium due to a greater risk, e.g. young drivers get loadings.

- **No claims bonus:** A reduction in the premium as a result of the insured not having made any previous claims.
- **Policy:** The official copy of the insurance contract between the insured and the insurance company. It contains all details of the insurance cover.
- **Premium:** The fee paid for insurance cover. It is based on the value of the item and the risk involved.
- **Proposal form:** The application form that the person seeking insurance fills in. When filling in this form, the principle of utmost good faith must be followed.

TAXATION

Types of household taxes

- **Pay As You Earn (PAYE):** The tax paid by individuals on money earned from working, also called income tax. As of 2006, the two rates of PAYE are 20 per cent and 42 per cent.
- **Self-assessment income tax:** People who are self-employed calculate and pay their own tax during the year. An estimate, called a **preliminary tax**, is paid by 31 October each year.
- **Value Added Tax (VAT):** A tax paid by consumers on goods and services they buy. There are two rates of VAT.
- **Motor tax:** A tax on motor vehicles, paid to the local authority.
- **Deposit Interest Retention Tax (DIRT):** Tax on interest earned on savings in a financial institution. The bank deducts it directly. As of 2006, the rate is 23 per cent.
- **Stamp duty:** A tax charged on the purchase of property. Different rates apply to different property values.

Taxes paid by business

- **Corporation tax:** Companies pay this tax on the profits they make. As of 2006, the corporation tax rate is 12.5 per cent.
- **VAT:** Businesses must pay VAT on purchases they make and charge it on sales. At the end of every two months they settle up with the Revenue, i.e. they break even.
- **PAYE:** Businesses deduct income tax from their employees and forward it to the Inland Revenue.
- **Motor tax:** This applies to businesses as well as households.
- **Capital gains tax:** If the business makes a profit on the sale of a fixed asset, it must pay tax on the profit made. This applies to households as well.
- **Customs/import duties:** These are charged on goods imported into the country from non-EU countries.

Tax forms

- **P12:** Employees fill this in and send it off to claim their tax credits. Until it is returned, a person pays emergency tax.
- **P45:** The employer gives this to the employee if he/she leaves work during the tax year. It shows gross income paid to the employee during that tax year and total tax deducted by the employer. It is given to the new employer by the employee or can be used to claim social welfare.
- **P60:** This is given by the employer to the employee at the end of the tax year. It shows the gross wage paid to the employee and the total tax and PRSI deducted during the year. This form is often used by the employee when seeking a loan/mortgage.
- **P21:** This is also called a **balancing statement**. If the employee feels that they have overpaid tax during the year, they send off for this form to seek a rebate of tax overpaid.

Tax credits and income tax calculations

Tax credits are the part of a person's income on which they are not taxed. Every PAYE worker is allowed to earn a certain amount of money without being taxed on it. A tax credit reduces the amount of tax that a person pays.

As of 2006, a single person has a personal tax credit of €1,630 and a PAYE tax credit of €1,490.

Table 4.3: Tax table from 1 January 2006

	Tax bands	**Tax credits**
Single person	• First €32,000 taxed at 20%. • Balance taxed at 42%.	• Personal tax credit of €1,630. • PAYE tax credit of €1,490.
Married couple (one spouse earning)	• First €41,000 taxed at 20%. • Balance taxed at 42%.	• Two personal tax credits of €1,630 each (total €3,260). • One PAYE credit of €1,490.
Married couple (both spouses earning and assuming joint assessment)	• First €64,000 taxed at 20%. • Balance taxed at 42%.	• Two personal tax credits of €1,630 each (total €3,260). • Two PAYE credits of €1,490 each (total €2,980).

TOTAL TAX – TAX CREDITS = TAX PAYABLE

Sample question 1

Calculate Paul's tax payable and monthly take-home pay if he earns a salary of €50,000 per annum. PRSI is 5 per cent of gross.

Solution

		€	€	€
Gross salary				50,000
Tax	€32,000 at 20%		6,400	
	€18,000 at 42%		7,560	
			13,960	
Less tax credits	Personal:	1,630		
	PAYE:	1,490		
			(3,120)	
Tax payable			10,840	
PRSI	5% of 50,000		2,500	(13,340)
Annual take-home				36,660
Monthly take-home				3,055

Sample Question 2

Jim and Joan are a married couple. Jim has a salary of €50,000 per annum. Joan works in the home. Calculate Jim's tax payable and monthly take-home pay. PRSI is 5 per cent of gross.

Solution

		€	€	€
Gross salary				50,000
Tax	€41,000 at 20%		8,200	
	€9,000 at 42%		3,780	
			11,980	
Less tax credits	Personal × 2	3,260		
	PAYE	1,490	4,750	
Tax payable			7,230	
PRSI			2,500	(9,730)
Annual take-home				40,270
Monthly take-home				3,356

Exam Tip: If asked to do a tax calculation question, all information will be supplied.

Common activities in managing a household and a business

TABLE 4.4: ACTIVITIES COMMON BETWEEN A HOUSEHOLD AND A BUSINESS

FINANCE	• Both budget and plan their spending by preparing cash flows and budgets. • Both use various banking services such as current and deposit accounts, bill payments, internet banking, etc. • Both keep records of their financial affairs.
INSURANCE	• Both take out insurance cover against a variety of risks. • Both fill out insurance forms, e.g. proposal and claim forms. • Both try to reduce premiums by reducing risks, e.g. fire.
TAXATION	• Both must pay taxes. Households pay PAYE and VAT, while companies pay corporation tax. • Both complete relevant tax forms. • Both try to reduce their tax liabilities, e.g. households can write off medical expenses, while businesses can write off interest payments.
GENERAL	• Both apply the management activities of planning, organising and controlling to their affairs.

Activities that differ in managing a household and a business

TABLE 4.5: ACTIVITIES THAT DIFFER BETWEEN A HOUSEHOLD AND A BUSINESS

FINANCE	• There is more finance flowing through a business than a household. • Businesses are required by law to keep financial records, whereas households are not. • When seeking finance, a business must supply much more information to the bank than a household, e.g. the past year's accounts.
INSURANCE	• Businesses need a much wider range of policies than households, e.g. public and employers' liability, consequential loss, etc. • Businesses can treat insurance premiums as an expense to reduce taxes; households cannot. • A business will suffer greater losses than a household.
TAXATION	• Businesses collect and pay more taxes than households, e.g. corporation tax, VAT. • A business can claim back VAT paid, whereas a household cannot. • Businesses act as unpaid tax collectors for the government. Households pay their own taxes directly.
GENERAL	• Scale of activities: Finances, insurance and taxes are dealt with on a far greater scale in a business than in a household. • Motivating factor: The motive in running a business is to make a profit, whereas there is no such motive in a household. • Legislation: Business is subject to much legislation, e.g. company law, health and safety laws. Households are not subject to as much legislation.

EXAM QUESTIONS

Exam question 1

Outline the activities common to and the activities different in managing a household and in managing a business. (20 marks)

Marking scheme
The scheme calls for **two** activities that are common and **two** activities that are different at **5 marks** each. The 5 marks are split into **2 marks** for naming the activity and **3 marks** for stating how it is common/different.

Sample answer
Common activities:
- **Finance (2 marks):** Both businesses and households keep records of their finances. Both budget and plan their spending and both use various banking services such as current and deposit accounts and online banking. **(3 marks)**
- **Insurance (2 marks):** Both businesses and households take out a variety of insurance. Both fill in insurance forms such as proposal and claim forms. Both try to reduce premiums by reducing risks. **(3 marks)**

Different activities:
- **Taxation (2 marks):** Businesses pay more taxes than households. Businesses can claim back VAT, whereas households cannot. Businesses can avail of certain tax allowances that households cannot. **(3 marks)**
- **Legislation (2 marks):** Business is subject to much legislation that households are not, e.g. company law, health and safety laws and competition laws. **(3 marks)**

4.2: HUMAN RESOURCE MANAGEMENT

FUNCTIONS OF HUMAN RESOURCE MANAGEMENT

1. Manpower planning

Manpower planning involves making sure the right staff with the right skills are employed in the firm, both now and in the future. It involves the following.
- **Human resource audit:** Looking at the skills presently available in the firm.
- **Human resource forecasting:** Predicting future labour needs.
- **Having a plan** about how to reduce or increase staff numbers as necessary, e.g. if a firm wanted to reduce staff, then retiring workers would not be replaced (natural wastage).

2. Recruitment and selection

Recruiting means finding applicants for jobs, while selection means choosing the successful applicants. The HR manager organises the following.

- **Job description:** This describes the work involved and the responsibilities attached to the job.
- **Person specification:** This describes the qualities that the successful candidate should have, including qualifications and experience.
- **Job advertisement:** Applicants that reply to the advertisement can be narrowed down (**screened**) and a smaller number **short listed** for an interview.
- **Interview:** The candidate who is successful in the interview will be offered a contract of employment.

A vacancy in a firm can be filled internally or externally.

TABLE 4.6: INTERNAL AND EXTERNAL RECRUITMENT

BENEFITS OF INTERNAL RECRUITMENT	BENEFITS OF EXTERNAL RECRUITMENT
• Improves morale in the firm. • Cheaper, as there are less training and recruitment expenses. • The person knows how the firm operates. • Avoids any resentment that may arise if an outsider got the job.	• New skills and ideas can be brought to the firm. • The best person can be chosen. • Avoids any jealousy as a result of an internal appointment. • May bring important business contacts.

3. Training and development

- **Induction training:** Introductory training that the worker gets when first starting the job. The aim is to make the employee familiar with the firm and to introduce him/her to colleagues.
- **On-the-job training:** This training takes place in the workplace. Other experienced staff members usually carry it out.
- **Off-the-job training:** This takes place outside the firm and normally involves training courses and in-service days.
- **Development:** This involves developing the whole person as opposed to just teaching the worker the skills of the job. Development prepares employees for promotions in the future.

4. Teamwork

The building of a team involves the stages of **forming, storming, norming** and **performing**.

TABLE 4.7: BENEFITS OF TEAMWORK

BENEFITS TO THE ORGANISATION	BENEFITS TO THE EMPLOYEE
• Improved decision making because of a wider range of views and experiences. • Motivation is improved, as employees know that they have an input. • Job satisfaction is improved, which reduces labour turnover and absenteeism. • Teams reveal leaders and the firm may find candidates for promotions.	• Morale is improved and workers are happier, as they are more involved. • Employees can offer each other encouragement and support. • Team members can learn new skills and get ideas from each other. • Teams allow employees to learn leadership skills and become eligible for promotions.

Possible drawbacks of teamwork

- Strong personalities can start to dominate the team. Quieter members may not get heard.
- Decision making can be slow due to everyone having to agree on certain issues.
- Personality clashes may emerge.

5. Performance appraisal

This is an assessment of the employee's performance in the job. It usually takes the form of an interview between the employee and the HR manager.

- The purpose of the appraisal is to **review and assess** the employee's performance over a period of time.
- The performance appraisal can be used as a means of determining **promotion**.
- It can be used as a means of deciding on a **reward system** in the firm. For example, bonuses or pay rises can be offered to employees who have achieved certain targets.
- The appraisal can be a **motivating tool** for the employee. If workers know they will be assessed regularly, this should motivate them to try to reach targets set for them.

6. *Reward*

Rewards given to employees can be financial or non-financial.

Financial rewards

- **Wage/salary:** Employees are either employed on an annual salary basis or a weekly wage. Payment may be time rate (hours worked), piece rate (amount produced) or commission (amount sold).
- **Bonus:** This is an extra payment as a reward for meeting a target.
- **Profit-sharing schemes:** Employees are paid a certain percentage of the profits that are over a certain amount.
- **Share ownership:** Free shares are given to the employees, often instead of a bonus.
- **Share options:** The employees are given the option of owning shares in the company at a preferential price.

Non-financial rewards

- **Benefits in kind:** These are also called 'perks'. Examples include a company car, subsidised meals, holidays and insurance.
- **Improved working conditions:** Employees may be rewarded with a shorter working week or flexitime.
- **Job enrichment:** This involves making the workplace a pleasant place to work. Workers are praised for work well done, given responsibility and allowed to use their initiative.
- **Job enlargement:** Increasing the variety of tasks a worker does in order to reduce boredom.

7. *Employer/employee relations*

The HR manager has an important role to play in establishing good industrial relations:
- Ensuring that good **communications** exist with staff. Communications should be open and honest.
- Ensuring **agreed procedures** exist for dealing with disputes. A good relationship with the shop steward is essential.
- Making sure staff are **consulted** on important issues concerning them, e.g. changes in work practices, possible redundancies.
- Looking after employees' **health, safety and welfare**.
- Having regular meetings with the **shop steward** to smooth over any industrial relations problems.

> **Exam Tip:** In a general question on the functions of the human resource manager, it would be unlikely a student would need to list any more than **five** functions. However, be aware that a question could be asked on one of the individual functions, e.g. teamwork, reward.

EXAM QUESTIONS

Exam question 1

Outline the benefits of teamwork to the employees of a business organisation. (20 marks)

Marking scheme

This is one of those questions where you might not be sure if it is four points at 5 marks each or five points at 4 marks each. If it appears difficult to get five points on a topic, then the scheme may well be only looking for four. In this case the scheme was **four** points at **5 marks** each. The breakdown is **3 marks** for the introduction of the point and **2 marks** for the development (extra point included).

Sample answer

- Workers' morale is improved through teamwork. **(3 marks)** When people work together, morale and motivation is improved, as everyone is working towards a common goal. **(2 marks)**
- Employees feel more involved in a team. **(3 marks)** As individuals, workers often feel unimportant and unnoticed, but in a team every member's contribution is important. **(2 marks)**
- Team members can learn new skills and ideas from each other. **(3 marks)** Everyone has skills and talents and these can be shared with other members of the team. **(2 marks)**
- Responsibility is shared in a team. **(3 marks)** Often people do not like making individual decisions, because if they do not work out, one person is responsible. In a team, the responsibility is spread out. **(2 marks)**
- Teams allow those with leadership skills to emerge. **(3 marks)** Thus, those employees with leadership skills can become promotion candidates. **(2 marks)**

4.3: CHANGING ROLE OF MANAGEMENT

CHANGES AFFECTING MANAGEMENT

- **Technology:** The increasing use of technology has meant that some workers can now work from home. This means less direct involvement with management.
- **Changing trends and fashions:** Due to TV advertising and rapid advances in product development, many products have shorter life cycles. Management has to respond very quickly to these changes.
- **Better-educated workforces:** Employees are very well trained and educated. This removes the need for management to be experts in all areas and in some ways allows staff to be their own bosses.

- **Bigger businesses:** Firms are increasing in size to take advantage of economies of scale. As a result, management structures are changing and more delegation is necessary.
- **Environmental issues:** Firms have many environmental responsibilities and it is management's role to ensure national and EU laws are obeyed.

IMPACT OF TECHNOLOGY ON THE ROLE OF MANAGEMENT

Impact on personnel

- The need for fewer employees has led to **redundancies**. This creates a need for employees to retrain and learn new skills.
- Technology allows some jobs to be done from outside the firm, as **location** has become less important. This allows some staff to work from home or other locations.
- Management and staff need more **training** to work with new IT developments. Constant retraining is required.
- The **type of employment** has changed. Jobs in the primary and secondary sectors have decreased, while employment in the service industry, which involves a lot of IT work, has increased.
- **Female employment** has increased due to the change from manual manufacturing and primary-sector work to a services-led economy.

Impact on business costs

- Costs may increase initially as firms need to install **new technologies**. There is a high capital cost of buying and maintaining the technology.
- Staff have to be **trained** in the use of the new systems. Constant retraining is also needed, which is expensive.
- Technology reduces the number of workers required. As a result, **wage costs** can be cut.
- New technologies will create redundancies. **Redundancy packages** will have to be paid to staff who are laid off.
- Management costs can be cut due to **video conferencing**, which allows meetings to take place from venues anywhere in the world without the need to travel.

Impact on business opportunities

- Information technology improves **efficiency** in a firm. The same work can now be done with fewer employees.
- Applications such as computer-aided design (CAD) and computer-aided manufacturing (CAM) improve the **design** process and increase productivity.
- Firms can carry out **market research** on markets and products from all over the world by using the internet.

- The internet allows firms to advertise and sell goods and services online. This is called **e-business**.
- As a result of IT, many firms now **recruit** staff over the internet. There are many recruitment websites available.

CHANGING ROLE OF MANAGER FROM CONTROLLER TO FACILITATOR

Controller manager

Traditionally in a company, the manager controlled everything that happened in the firm. The manager gave orders and expected them to be carried out with no questions asked. He/she was an expert in all aspects of the business. Employees had no real say in the decision-making process. Most managers were autocratic managers.

As society and business changed, however, managers realised that they could not do everything and their style of management had to change.

Facilitator manager

The modern manager must accept change as natural and help bring it about. This can be done in the following ways.

- **Resources:** Provide the resources necessary for staff to become empowered. This involves time and money.
- **Facilitating:** Allow the staff to achieve what they are capable of. Any barriers to staff achieving their potential should be removed.
- **Consulting:** Staff members should be consulted regularly. Staff's knowledge and experience are vital to the business.
- **Mentoring:** Senior members of staff should be used as coaches to less senior members.

The role of the manager has changed from being a controller manager to being a **coach**, **resource provider** and **facilitator**.

EMPOWERMENT

Empowerment means placing real power and responsibility in the hands of the workers. Workers are allowed to make their own decisions and use their initiative in carrying out their duties. Empowerment is more than delegation, since delegation sets limits on the responsibility passed to the employees. With empowerment, workers are responsible for making decisions and exercising control.

Requirements for empowerment to take place

- **Training:** Empowerment is difficult and employees and management need training in how to implement it.
- **Management support:** Employees must be assured that management is in favour of staff empowerment.
- **Consultation:** The manager must consult the staff regularly. Staff suggestions and recommendations must be taken seriously.
- **Mentoring:** Managers must be prepared to become advisors to staff members. Being a mentor means acting as a coach and guide to employees.

Benefits of empowerment to the organisation

- The **quality** of the work is improved, as workers' talents are unlocked.
- The service to customers is greatly improved, which should **increase sales** and profits.
- Staff **motivation and morale** are improved, as workers know that management takes their opinions seriously.
- **Absenteeism** and labour turnover should be reduced as workers develop a sense of loyalty to the organisation.
- When employees are given responsibility, leaders should emerge and **promotions** can be filled from within.

TOTAL QUALITY MANAGEMENT (TQM)

TQM is a concentrated and continuous effort by management to create a culture of quality throughout the organisation. The Japanese developed this system of management.

Principles of and requirements for TQM

- **Satisfying customer needs:** Companies survive and make profits because of customers. Therefore, it is important for businesses to listen to their customers and satisfy their needs.
- **Continuous improvement:** All businesses must continuously improve products and processes. If a firm does not do things better each year, then a competitor will.
- **Total company involvement (teamwork):** Teams are more creative in their approach to problem solving and idea generation, and as a result, better-quality decisions are made.
- **Benchmarking:** This involves firms comparing themselves to the very best businesses and trying to reach the same high standards of quality.
- **Zero defects:** This means eliminating faults in goods and services. Defects are costly and time consuming to correct. The aim of TQM is to get production and delivery right first time.

- **Empowerment:** Workers must be given responsibility and the freedom to become their own quality controllers. They are closest to the customers and are often the first to see the need for improvements.

> **Exam Tip:** It is not necessary for you to know all of the above points. Also, there are other aspects of TQM that you could use, such as **Q Mark**, **quality circles**, **ISO**, **just-in-time**, etc. These have been covered in Unit 3.3 as part of quality control.

Benefits of TQM

- Quality of goods and services is improved, and as a result, **sales and profits** increase.
- Firms that get a reputation for quality can charge **higher prices** for their goods and services.
- **Costs** are reduced, as there is less wastage due to fewer errors. This results from a policy of getting it right first time.
- Staff become more motivated and **morale improves** as employees feel they are a part of the improvements in quality.
- Firms that adopt a TQM approach improve their chances of getting ISO recognition, which in turn enhances their reputation in the **export markets**.

STRATEGIES FOR MANAGING CHANGE

- **Consultation:** Management needs to consult the staff and their unions on changes, because if change is forced on staff without consultation, they will probably resist it.
- **Communication:** Constant communication is needed between management and staff. Open and honest communication will eliminate any fears the workers have.
- **Negotiation:** Trade unions will want to negotiate on behalf of the workers on the benefits that change will bring in relation to productivity improvements and possible increased profits. Pay rises may be sought.
- Create a **culture of change:** If management puts across the idea that change is good and everyone benefits from it, then a culture of change will be accepted in the firm.
- **Training:** Training must be provided to both the management and staff in order for them to understand what is involved in the process of change. Funding must be provided for this training.

EXAM QUESTIONS

> ### Exam question 1
>
> *Discuss the importance of total quality management (TQM) to a business enterprise.* (20 marks)
>
> **Marking scheme**
> **Four** points at **5 marks** each. The 5 marks are split into **2 marks** for introducing the point and **3 marks** for developing the point.
>
> **Sample answer**
> - TQM improves the quality of the firm's goods and services. **(2 marks)** This will have the effect of increasing the firm's sales and profits. **(3 marks)**
> - Due to a TQM approach, a firm's costs will be reduced. **(2 marks)**. This will be the result of less waste due to fewer errors. The firm now has a policy of getting it right first time. **(3 marks)**
> - Morale and motivation will be improved in the firm. **(2 marks)** This is because a TQM approach involves all staff members. All employees feel that their efforts are appreciated and noticed. **(3 marks)**
> - Any business involved in the export trade will benefit from a TQM approach. **(2 marks)** Getting a reputation for quality and perhaps ISO recognition will create a good impression with foreign firms. **(3 marks)**

4.4: MONITORING THE BUSINESS

USERS OF FINANCIAL INFORMATION

- **Management:** Will want information to know how the business has performed over the year and to learn if any changes are needed.
- **Shareholders:** They will want to know if the money that they have invested has been used wisely by the firm in order to generate profits and pay them a dividend.
- **Banks:** Will want to know if the firm has been profitable enough to make loan repayments and interest payments.
- **Trade unions:** Keep an eye on company profits because if the business is doing very well, then a wage increase may be sought.
- **Competitors:** Will examine sales and profits to get an idea of how big a threat the firm is to them.
- **Suppliers:** Are interested in the company accounts in order to assess if the firm can pay for goods supplied on credit.

FINANCIAL STATEMENTS

Trading, profit and loss account

- The **trading account** shows the sales, purchases, cost of sales and gross profit of the firm.
- The **profit and loss account** shows the total expenses, such as insurance, rent and rates, light and heat and wages. It shows the net profit (profit after expenses), the dividend paid to the shareholders and the retained profit for the year.

Balance sheet

The balance sheet shows:
- **Fixed assets**, such as premises, machinery and equipment. The premises can be used as security for any loans the firm has.
- **Current assets**, such as stock, debtors, cash balances and amounts pre-paid by the firm.
- **Current liabilities**, such as creditors, bank overdrafts and amounts the firm owes.
- **Working capital**. This is the current assets minus the current liabilities. It measures the liquidity of the firm, i.e. the firm's ability to pay its short-term debts as they fall due.
- **Long-term liabilities:** These include share capital (authorised and issued), long-term loans and retained profits (profit and loss balances from previous years).

The **authorised share capital** is the maximum share capital that the company can raise.

The **issued share capital** is the actual amount of capital that has been raised from selling shares.

RATIOS

You need to know the following **six** ratios under **three** headings (profitability, liquidity and gearing ratios).

Profitability ratios

Gross margin (gross profit percentage)

$$\frac{\textbf{GROSS PROFIT}}{\textbf{SALES}} \times 100$$

This measures the percentage of each €1 of sales that is gross profit. It should be compared to the previous year. Reasons for a decline in this ratio would be a reduction in the selling price or an increase in the cost of purchases without a corresponding increase in the selling price.

Net margin (net profit percentage)

$$\frac{\text{NET PROFIT}}{\text{SALES}} \times 100$$

This measures the percentage of each €1 of sales that is net profit. It should be compared to the previous year. The main reason for a decline in this ratio is an increase in expenses.

Return on investment (ROI)

$$\frac{\text{NET PROFIT}}{\text{CAPITAL EMPLOYED}} \times 100$$

This ratio is also called the **return on capital employed (ROCE)**. This is a measure of how effectively the company has used its capital. It should be compared to the previous year. In addition, it should be well above (at least 5 per cent) the interest rate that could be earned in a deposit account.

Note: Be aware of interest rates on deposits in financial institutions.

Liquidity ratios

Current (working capital) ratio

$$\frac{\text{CURRENT ASSETS}}{\text{CURRENT LIABILITIES}} \times 100$$

This is a measure of a firm's liquidity, i.e. its ability to pay its short-term debts as they fall due. The recommended ratio is 2:1. This means that ideally the firm should have €2 to pay each €1 of debts owed in the short term.

Acid test (quick) ratio

$$\frac{\text{CURRENT ASSETS – CLOSING STOCKS}}{\text{CURRENT LIABILITIES}}$$

The recommended ratio is 1:1. This means that ideally the firm should have €1 of current assets, excluding closing stock, to pay each €1 of current liabilities owed.

If both these ratios are good, the firm is said to be **liquid.** If the ratios are below the recommended figures, then the firm may be experiencing liquidity problems. This can also be called **overtrading**.

Gearing ratio
Debt equity ratio

$$\frac{\text{DEBT CAPITAL}}{\text{EQUITY CAPITAL}} \times 100$$

DEBT CAPITAL = long-term loans (do not include overdrafts)
EQUITY = share capital + reserves

This measures the **gearing** of the firm, i.e. the relationship of loan (debt) capital to equity capital (share capital plus reserves). If the percentage is over 100 per cent, the firm is said to be **highly geared**. If the percentage is less than 100 per cent, the firm has **low gearing**. Low gearing is better for a business.

High gearing entails the following problems:
- Banks may be reluctant to lend more money to a firm that is highly geared.
- Shareholders may be unwilling to invest in a firm that has high gearing, as the chances of good dividends are reduced.
- Firms with high levels of borrowings are under financial pressure to make loan and interest payments.

EXAM QUESTIONS

Exam question 1

Illustrate the benefit for the good financial management of a business of the (a) profit and loss account and (b) balance sheet. (20 marks)

Marking scheme
Two points are required on each at **5 marks** each. The 5 marks are split into **3 marks** for the first piece of information and **2 marks** for a brief development of it.

Sample answer
- The profit and loss account contains a trading account section. This shows the sales and the cost of sales of the firm. **(3 marks)** The sales minus the cost of sales equals the gross profit. This is the profit before the expenses are deducted. **(2 marks)**
- The P and L account shows all the expenses and the net profit. **(3 marks)** At the end of the P and L account is the appropriation account, which shows the dividend for the year and the retained profit for the year. **(2 marks)**
- The balance sheet shows the firm's fixed and current assets. **(3 marks)** Fixed assets include premises and equipment, while current assets include stock and debtors. **(2 marks)**
- The balance sheet also shows the current and long-term liabilities. **(3 marks)** Current liabilities include creditors and bank overdrafts, while long-term liabilities include share capital, long-term loans and retained earnings. **(2 marks)**

Note: Other points could also be used here, such as gearing, liquidity, etc.

Exam question 2

(a) *Using two ratios in each case, analyse the profitability and liquidity trends in Down Under Ltd from the following figures for 2008 and 2009.*

(b) *Suggest how the trends might be improved.* (40 marks)

TABLE 4.8: ACCOUNTS OF DOWN UNDER LTD

	2008	2009
Current assets	45,000	48,000
Net profit	43,500	37,650
Equity share capital	300,000	320,000
Current liabilities	24,000	31,000
Closing stock	25,000	24,000
Gross profit	127,000	114,500
Retained earnings	45,000	49,400
Sales	467,000	443,000

Marking scheme

The scheme is **four** ratios at **10 marks** each. The 10 marks may be split into **2 marks** for writing out the formula, **3 marks** each for each year's calculations and **2 marks** for the comment.

Sample answer

TABLE 4.9: SOLUTION FOR DOWN UNDER LTD

PROFITABILITY	2008	2009
Gross margin = (gross profit ÷ sales) × 100 (**2 marks**)	$(127,000\mathbf{1m} \div 467,000\mathbf{1m})$ × 100 = 27.2%**1m**	$(114,500\mathbf{1m} \div 443,000\mathbf{1m})$ × 100 = 25.84%**1m**
Net margin = (net profit ÷ sales) × 100 (**2 marks**)	$(43,500\mathbf{1m} \div 467,000\mathbf{1m})$ × 100 = 9.3%**1m**	$(37,650\mathbf{1m} \div 443,000\mathbf{1m})$ × 100 = 8.5%**1m**
Return on investment = (net profit ÷ cap. employed) × 100 (**2 marks**)	$(43,500\mathbf{1m} \div 345,000\mathbf{1m})$ × 100 = 12.6%**1m**	$(37,650\mathbf{1m} \div 369,400\mathbf{1m})$ × 100 = 10.2%**1m**

LIQUIDITY	2008	2009
Working capital ratio = current assets ÷ current liabilities **(2 marks)**	45,000**1m** ÷ 24,000**1m** = 1.88:1 **1m**	48,000**1m** ÷ 31,000**1m** = 1.55:1 **1m**
Acid test ratio: (current assets – closing stock) ÷ current liabilities **(2 marks)**	(45,000 – 25,000)**1m** ÷ 24,000**1m** = .83:1 **1m**	(48,000 – 24,000) **1m** ÷ 31,000**1m** = .77:1 **1m**

- The gross margin has declined from 2008 to 2009. This ratio could be improved by more effective purchasing, i.e. sourcing cheaper materials. **(2 marks)**
- The net margin has fallen from 9.3 per cent to 8.5 per cent. This could be improved by the firm reducing its expenses. **(2 marks)**
- The ROI has fallen from 12.6 per cent to 10.2 per cent. The company needs to make more efficient use of its capital. Reducing expenses and/or increasing sales can achieve this. **(2 marks)**
- The current ratio has fallen from 1.88:1 to 1.55:1. This is below the recommended 2:1. Liquidity can be improved by better credit control. **(2 marks)**
- The acid test ratio has fallen from .83:1 to .77:1. This is below the recommended 1:1. **(2 marks)**

IMPORTANT DEFINITIONS FROM UNIT 4

- **Cash flow forecast:** An estimate of a firm's projected future inflows and outflows. It is used by the firm as a planning tool.
- **Average clause:** This rule states that if an item is underinsured and a partial loss occurs, then the insured will only get the same fraction of the damage as that fraction of its value for which the item was insured.
- **Risk management:** A planned approach to the handling of risk. It involves the identification and assessment of risks and then trying to minimise them.
- **Tax credits:** Deductions from a person's gross tax. Every PAYE worker has two basic tax credits: a personal credit and a PAYE credit.
- **Direct tax:** A tax that is taken directly from a person's wage. PAYE is an example of a direct tax.
- **Indirect tax:** This is not taken directly from the taxpayer. VAT, which is a tax on spending, is an indirect tax.
- **Self-assessment:** The tax system that applies to the self-employed. Self-employed people calculate and pay their own taxes during the year.
- **Manpower planning:** An assessment of the business's current and future labour needs. It involves doing a human resource audit and human resource forecasting.
- **Job description:** This describes the work involved and the responsibilities attached to the job that is being advertised.
- **Person specification:** This describes the qualities that the successful candidate should have for the job. It includes qualifications, experience and personal characteristics.
- **Performance appraisal:** An assessment of the employee's performance in the job. It is carried out by the HR manager and usually takes the form of an interview.
- **E-business:** This is when firms conduct business over the internet. Advertising takes place via a website. Firms sell their goods and services online.
- **Empowerment:** This involves management placing real power and responsibility in the hands of the workers. Empowerment is much more than delegation, since the employees are allowed to use their initiative in doing their jobs.
- **Total quality management (TQM):** A concentrated and continuous effort by management to create a culture of quality throughout the organisation. The aim of TQM is to get it right first time and to avoid defects.
- **Working capital:** The current assets minus the current liabilities. It is the finance available for the day-to-day running of the firm.
- **Liquidity:** A measure of the firm's ability to pay its short-term debts as they fall due. It is measured by the current ratio and the acid test ratio.
- **Gearing:** This measures the extent to which a firm is financed by debt capital (loans) as opposed to equity capital (share capital plus reserves). Low gearing is better for a company, as there is less financial risk.

CHAPTER 5
Unit 5: Business in Action

5.1: IDENTIFYING OPPORTUNITIES

GENERATING IDEAS

Idea generation in a business should be a systematic and deliberate approach.

Internal sources of ideas

- **Research and development (R&D) department:** Most big companies have their own R&D department that is constantly researching new product ideas, e.g. Glanbia.
- **Sales personnel:** Salespeople will often come back with ideas from retailers or customers that may be turned into successful products.
- **Employees:** Some firms encourage intrapreneurship and reward employees who come up with ideas for new products or services.
- **Brainstorming:** These are idea generation sessions held between staff and management. Most ideas will be rejected, but some will be given further consideration.
- **SWOT analysis:** A SWOT analysis may lead to weaknesses being improved and possible new ideas developed.

External sources of ideas

- **Competitors:** If a rival company comes up with a new idea, then other companies will produce a version of the product.
- **Customers:** Customer requirements and suggestions can be a good source of new ideas. If enough customers demand something, then there is a gap/niche in the market for it.
- **Market trends:** If companies keep abreast of changes in society, this will create openings for new products and services.
- **Abroad:** Businesspeople often travel to trade fairs in other countries or may spot ideas when away on foreign trips or holidays.

- **Market research agencies:** Market research agencies do research in different areas and then sell this information in return for a fee.
- **State agencies:** Government agencies such as Enterprise Ireland, or at a local level the County Enterprise Boards, can help firms to come up with new ideas or new markets for their products.

NEW PRODUCT AND SERVICE DEVELOPMENT PROCESS

1. Product screening

This is the process of separating weak ideas from stronger ones. A firm needs to eliminate poor ideas as soon as possible so as to not lose money developing them. At this stage, the firm will ask the following questions:
- Does the product fill a customer need?
- Does the firm have the skills and resources to make it?
- Does it fit in with the firm's existing products?
- Will the product be profitable to produce?

2. Concept development

At the concept development stage, the idea is now made more precise.

A product concept is a precise statement of the need the product will fill and the form that it will take.

Questions answered at this stage are:
- What will the product actually look like?
- What will it do for the customer?

3. Feasibility study

This is a study (research) carried out on the product/service to see if it would be viable both commercially and technically.

The following information will be sought:
- Does the firm have the necessary skills to make it?
- How much will it cost to make and can the firm afford it?
- How will it impact on existing products/services?

4. Prototype development

A prototype is a first working example of a product from which subsequent copies are made or from which improved specimens are developed.

- It proves that the product can actually be made.
- It identifies any problems with the product.
- It shows the actual appearance of the product.

5. Test marketing

Test marketing involves testing the reaction of a small group of people to a product before going into full production with it.

By testing the product on a small target market first, the risk of failure is greatly reduced. Customer reaction to the product is taken on board and improvements and changes can be made. A decision is now made on whether or not to launch the product into full production.

6. Production and launch

If the test marketing results are positive, the firm will go into full-scale production. The product will start off at the introduction stage of the product life cycle.

> **Exam Tip:** When answering a question on the new product or service development process, be sure to give an example of a product or service. Make a reference to this product/service at **each stage** of the process. Make sure the steps are in the correct order.

MARKET RESEARCH

Market research is the collecting, recording and detailed examination of all data dealing with the transfer of goods from the producer to the consumer.

Reasons for market research

- Market research **reduces the risk** of products failing. When developing a new product, a firm will do research at various stages of the development.
- It provides **information** on the company's **target market**. This is the group of people who are most likely to buy the firm's products. The firm can then develop a product to suit their needs.
- It provides information on **competitors**. This helps a firm to identify its competitors' strengths and weaknesses and to try to increase market share.
- It helps the firm to **set prices** for its products and services by identifying the target market and its spending power.
- It can be used to find out why a product is **not selling**. The company can then take action to rectify this.
- It can be used to test **customer reaction** to a product or service.

Types of market research

Desk research

This is the sourcing of information that is already available. It is taken from the internet, sales publications, Central Statistics Office reports, etc. It is often referred to as **secondary** information and by itself is not enough to base any major decisions on.

Field research

This is where the information is collected by going out into the marketplace (the field). This is called **primary** research. It is more accurate than desk research, as the opinions of the target market can be sought. There are various methods of field research:

- **Questionnaires:** A sample of the public is selected to answer a number of questions.
- **Personal interviews:** People are surveyed on the street or at their homes.
- **Telephone surveys:** Customers are contacted by telephone and asked for their opinions on a certain product or service.

EXAM QUESTIONS

Exam question 1

Define the term 'feasibility study'. (10 marks)

Marking scheme

A short question like this usually requires **two** pieces of information.

Sample answer

This is a study carried out to assess the commercial viability of a new product. **(5 marks)** It is one of the stages of the new product development process and lets the firm know if it should proceed. **(5 marks)**

Exam question 2

Explain the stages involved in the development process of a new product or service of your choice. (30 marks)

Marking scheme

The marking scheme requires **five** stages at **6 marks** each. The 6 marks is split into **2 marks** for naming the stage, **2 marks** for a piece of information on the stage and **2 marks** for tying in an example each time.

Sample answer

- **Idea generation (2 marks):** This means coming up with new ides for the business. Ideas may come from internal or external sources. **(2 marks)** For example, McDonald's is always thinking about new product ideas. **(2 marks)**
- **Product screening (2 marks):** This is when the strong ideas are separated from the weaker ones. The firm asks if the product can be made and if it will be a profitable addition to their product range. **(2 marks)** When McDonald's was coming up with ideas for healthy options to their range, they abandoned many ideas at an early stage. **(2 marks)**
- **Concept development (2 marks):** This is when the idea is made more specific. The firm decides what the product will actually look like and the exact role it will fill for the customer. **(2 marks)** McDonald's decided that they would offer salad options in plastic cases. **(2 marks)**
- **Feasibility study (2 marks):** This is research carried out on the idea to assess if it would be both commercially and technically viable. The firm does a cost-benefit analysis. **(2 marks)** McDonald's calculated the costs of making the salads and the possible sales they would generate. **(2 marks)**
- **Prototype development (2 marks):** This is the first working model of the product. It shows what the product looks like and identifies any problems it may have. **(2 marks)** McDonald's made a succession of prototypes of the salads and improved them each time. **(2 marks)**

5.2: MARKETING

Marketing is the process of identifying, anticipating and satisfying the needs of consumers and making a profit doing it.

MARKETING CONCEPT

The marketing concept involves identifying and satisfying customer needs profitably. The firm puts the customer first and tries to have the right products in the right places at the right prices. A firm that uses the marketing concept is said to have a **marketing orientation**. The benefits of adopting the marketing concept are:

- Business sales and profits will be strong since the firm is producing what customers want.
- In very competitive markets, companies will retain their market share.

Marketing strategy and marketing plan

The marketing strategy is the long-term marketing approach the firm takes to achieve its marketing objectives. The following elements are involved.

- **SWOT analysis:** A firm will first look at its strengths and weaknesses in the marketplace. A **strength** might be a strong sales team, while a **weakness** may be a small product range. An **opportunity** might be widening the product range and a **threat** might be a new competitor.
- **Market research:** The collecting, recording and detailed examination of all data relating to the transfer of goods from the producer to the consumer.
- **Market segmentation:** Companies break the market up into segments. Each different segment is known as a **target market**. Segmentation can be done on the basis of age, gender, disposable income, religion or ethnic groups, family status, etc. Once the different segments are known, the firm can adopt a different marketing approach to each segment.
- **Marketing mix:** This is also known as the four Ps of marketing: product, price, promotion and place.

Advantages of a marketing strategy/plan

- By its very nature, the plan requires setting **goals**. These goals can then be compared with actual performance to assess if they have been achieved.
- A marketing plan is used along with a business plan when the firm is seeking **finance** from the government or a financial institution.
- A marketing plan focuses the whole firm on developing the **marketing mix**.

DEVELOPING THE MARKETING MIX (THE FOUR PS)

The marketing mix is the set of tactics the firm uses to achieve its marketing objectives. There are four elements to the marketing mix: product, price, promotion and place.

PRODUCT

There are a number of different aspects to a product.

- **Research and development:** Most large manufacturing firms have an R&D department that tries to make improvements to existing products and come up with ideas for new products.
- **Design:** The product must look good, be safe and be easy to use. Products must now satisfy EU regulations on design as well as Irish ones. The designer of a new product can take out a patent, which prevents anyone else from copying it.
- **Packaging:** Packaging is often regarded as a fifth P of marketing. The packaging is what the customer sees first, so it must be attractive and eye catching. A package should be recyclable and obey the laws in relation to important information, etc.

- **Branding: Branding is the marking of goods with a distinguishing name, mark or symbol which allows customers to instantly recognise it**, e.g. the Mercedes sign, the Nike 'swoosh', etc. Benefits or branding are as follows.
  - ➤ **Differentiates** the firm's products from other similar products.
  - ➤ Makes products easy to **identify**.
  - ➤ Customers often develop a sense of **loyalty** towards a brand name.
  - ➤ Branded goods can sometimes be sold at **higher prices** because of an image of quality associated with them.
  - ➤ Branding is essential if a firm is involved in **global marketing**.

Product life cycle

These are the stages that a product goes through from its development to its decline and removal from the marketplace. All products have a life cycle.

FIGURE 5.1: PRODUCT LIFE CYCLE

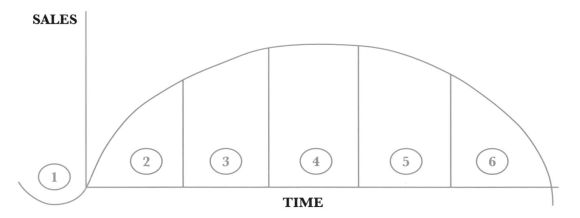

1. **Development:** The majority of the costs of the product are incurred here on areas such as feasibility studies, prototype developments, etc.
2. **Introduction:** The product is launched onto the market. A lot of money is spent on advertising and promoting it. Sales are slow.
3. **Growth:** Sales start to grow as more people get to know about the product.
4. **Maturity:** Sales start to level off as the firm struggles to attract more customers. Competition is intense.
5. **Saturation:** Sales start to fall as competitors fight back. Money has to be spent on advertising to keep existing customers.
6. **Decline:** The product has now run its course, as customers are tired of it. The firm must reinvent the product or else take it off the market.

PRICE

Factors to consider when deciding on the price

- What the product **cost** to develop and make.
- What the **competitors** are charging.
- What type of customer makes up the **target market**.
- **Special features** of the product, e.g. added extras on new cars.
- **Seasonal** influences, e.g. end of summer season.

Pricing strategies

- **Cost plus pricing:** The firm considers all the costs involved in getting the product to the market. Then it adds on a profit margin.
- **Premium pricing:** Some customers are prepared to pay more for what they see as higher quality, e.g. expensive restaurants.
- **Penetration pricing:** This involves going in with a low price to try to gain market share. Higher volumes of sales will compensate for the low profit margins.
- **Price skimming:** This involves charging as high a price as possible when demand is high in order to maximise profits, e.g. accommodation on holiday/international sporting weekends.
- **Below-cost selling:** Since the lifting of the ban on below-cost selling in 2006, some supermarkets sell certain products at less than cost price (loss leaders) in order to attract customers.

Break-even analysis

A break-even analysis is based on the assumption that manufacturing costs can be divided into variable costs and fixed costs.

- **Variable costs:** These costs vary in direct proportion to the quantity of goods produced, e.g. if production doubles, these costs will double. The two main variable costs are materials and labour.
- **Fixed costs:** These costs stay the same regardless of the amount produced (within a certain range). Examples include rent, rates and a manager's salary.
- **Total costs** are fixed plus variable.
- **Break-even point:** The level of sales at which the firm neither makes a profit nor a loss.

> **Contribution =** selling price − variable cost
>
> **Break-even =** $\dfrac{\text{fixed costs}}{\text{contribution per unit}}$

- **Margin of safety:** The amount by which a firm's sales can fall (from the forecast level) before it starts to make a loss, i.e. before the break-even point is reached.

> Margin of safety = forecast output − break-even sales

Sample question

1. Wheelers manufactures exercise bicycles. It supplies the following information about its activities:

Fixed costs	€300,000
Variable cost per unit	€150
Forecasted output	5,000 units
Selling price per unit	€250

(a) Illustrate by means of a break-even chart: (i) break-even point (ii) profit at full capacity (iii) margin of safety.

(b) Outline the effect on the break-even point if variable costs increased to €170 per unit.

Exam Tip: Do the calculations first.

Solution

(a) (i) **Break-even** = $\dfrac{€300,000}{€100}$ = **3,000 units**

In sales revenue, this is 3,000 × €250 (selling price) = **€750,000**

(ii) **Profit at full capacity** = 5,000 (full capacity)

$\underline{(3,000)}$ (break-even)

2,000 (profit-making units) × €100 (profit per unit)

= **€200,000**

(iii) **Margin of safety** = 5,000 – 3,000 = **2,000 units**

(b) If variable costs increased to €170 per unit, then the contribution per unit will decrease to €80 (€250 – €170). The new break-even point will be €300,000 ÷ €80 = **3,750 units.** In sales revenue, it will be €937,500 (3750 x €250).

Steps in drawing a break-even chart

● The break-even point is 3,000 units, or €750,000. By doubling each of these we get 6,000 units and €1,500,000. Make these two figures the extreme points on the graph and scale back to the (0, 0) axis.

● Plot the break-even point.

● Plot the fixed costs line as a horizontal line from the vertical axis.

● Plot the total costs line from the fixed costs axis and through the break-even point.

● Plot the total revenue line from the (0, 0) axis and through the break-even.

FIGURE 5.2: BREAK-EVEN CHART

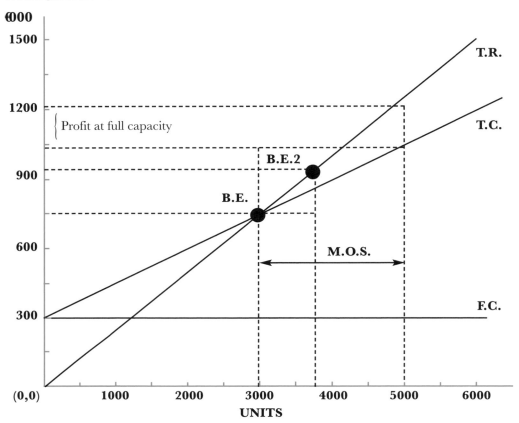

PROMOTION

Advertising

Advertising is the communication of information about a product or service to a firm's target market or the general public in order to maintain or increase sales.

Reasons for advertising

- Makes the public **aware** of new products coming onto the market.
- Informs the public about a product or service – **informative advertising**.
- Tries to increase sales by convincing the public that a product is better than others – **competitive advertising**.
- Reminds customers that a product is still available – **reminder advertising**.
- Attempts to **increase market share** at the expense of competitors.
- Tries to persuade the public that they cannot live without the product or service – **persuasive advertising**.

Advertising media include television, radio, newspapers, internet, billboards, cinema, commuter advertising, leaflets and flyers.

Sales promotion

Sales promotion involves all forms of promoting goods or services other than direct advertising or personal selling.

Examples of sales promotion include:
- Buy one get one free.
- Three for two offers.
- 33 per cent extra free.
- Free gifts with products.
- 50c off next purchase.
- Collecting a certain number of tokens.

Public relations

Public relations (PR) involves establishing and maintaining a good public image for a firm and its products in the hope of increasing sales.

Some large firms have their own public relations officer (PRO) while others employ the services of external PR agencies.

Public relations may involve:
- Press releases to the media.
- Dealing with customer complaints.
- Sponsorship of local events.
- Customer days.

Merchandising

Merchandising is the display of products at or near the point of sale in order to increase sales of the product. The manufacturer usually provides this service to the retailer.

Examples of merchandising are:
- Product displays in supermarkets.
- Food tasting in supermarkets.
- Window displays.

Direct marketing

Direct marketing involves contacting customers directly by telephone or mail to try to persuade them to buy something. Mail marketing involves putting promotional material through letterboxes, while telemarketing means contacting the person by phone, e.g. telephone companies trying to win new customers.

PLACE

Channels of distribution

Channels of distribution are the means by which the goods get from the manufacturer to the consumer. There are different channels suitable to different goods.

1. Manufacturer			$\rightarrow$ Consumer
2. Manufacturer		$\rightarrow$ Retailer	$\rightarrow$ Consumer
3. Manufacturer	$\rightarrow$ Wholesaler	$\rightarrow$ Retailer	$\rightarrow$ Consumer
4. Manufacturer	$\rightarrow$ Agent	$\rightarrow$ Retailer	$\rightarrow$ Consumer
5. Manufacturer	$\rightarrow$ Internet		$\rightarrow$ Consumer

The channel of distribution that is chosen will depend on whether or not:

- Goods are perishable – then channels 1 or 2 will be chosen.
- The goods are being imported – then an agent may be needed, e.g. channel 4.
- The retailer is large – then it will be able to deal directly with the manufacturer, e.g. channel 2.

Wholesaler

This is the link between the manufacturer and the retailer. The wholesaler buys in bulk from the manufacturer and sells in smaller quantities to the retailers. An example of a wholesaler is a cash and carry.

Retailer

This is the outlet that sells to the consumer in small quantities. Examples are all shops.

> **Exam Tip:** If asked to evaluate the elements of the marketing mix using a product or service of your choice, then make a reference to your product/service for **each of the four Ps**.

EXAM QUESTIONS

Exam question 1

Evaluate the elements of the marketing mix using a product or service of your choice. (30 marks)

Marking scheme
The scheme here is the four Ps at **8 marks, 8 marks, 7 marks and 7 marks**. The marks are split into **2 marks** for naming the 'P', **2 marks** for each example and **3/4 marks** for the piece of information.

Sample answer

The product chosen is Volvic flavoured water.

- **Product (2 marks):** A lot of research must go into the making of any new product. The product must be branded with a distinct name, sign or symbol. It will enter the product life cycle at the introduction stage. **(4 marks)** Volvic is a natural spring water with a variety of flavours. It was introduced to the market in 2006. **(2 marks)**
- **Price (2 marks):** The firm must decide on a price to charge. It must be roughly the same as competitors' and also cover all production costs. Some firms use strategies such as penetration and premium pricing. **(4 marks)** Volvic charges about 30c more per bottle for flavoured water. **(2 marks)**
- **Promotion (2 marks):** Launching a new product requires a lot of promotion. Methods include various advertising media, such as TV, radio and newspaper. Sales promotion can also be used, e.g. money off, buy one get one free, extra free. **(3 marks)** Volvic advertises on TV, e.g. a caveman drinks Volvic and escapes from dinosaurs. **(2 marks)**
- **Place (2 marks):** This involves the channels of distribution used to get the product from the manufacturer to the consumer, i.e. wholesaler, retailer. Methods of transport will also be considered here. **(3 marks)** Volvic is sold in all retail outlets. **(2 marks)**

5.3: GETTING STARTED

People start their own business for many reasons, such as independence, life-long ambition, family tradition, a challenge or perhaps as a result of redundancy, just to name a few.

FINANCE OPTIONS

There are **three** categories of finance: short, medium and long term.

Short term (up to one year)

- **Bank overdraft:** This is when current account holders can withdraw more money than they have in their account up to a certain limit that is pre-arranged with the bank. Interest is charged on the overdrawn amount.

- **Accrued expenses:** Expenses that a business has incurred but has not yet paid for.
- **Trade creditors:** Almost all firms buy stock on credit and pay for it at a later date (usually one to two months). In the meantime they have hopefully sold the stock and use the proceeds for other purposes in the business.
- **Factoring debtors:** This involves a firm factoring (selling) its debts to a factoring company or bank. The factoring company pays the firm a percentage of what they are owed from the debtors and then it collects the full amount from the debtors.

Medium term (one to five years)

- **Term loan:** A loan that carries a fixed rate of interest and has fixed repayment dates. It is usually used to purchase fixed assets such as machinery and equipment.
- **Hire purchase:** Instead of buying assets outright, many firms choose to buy them on hire purchase. Ownership passes to the firm only on the last payment.
- **Leasing:** Instead of buying outright, the firm rents the asset. As with hire purchase, rental payments can be offset against tax.

Long term (five years and over)

- **Ordinary share capital:** This involves the sale of shares (part-ownership) in the company to people willing to invest. The original owners of the company lose some control and have to pay a dividend to the shareholders. Share capital does not have to be repaid.
- **Long-term loans:** Bank loans usually secured on the assets of the business. The loan plus interest must be repaid. However, the interest portion of the loan can be written off against tax. Loans increase the **gearing** of the company.
- **Retained earnings/reserves:** Profits that the company has made in previous years and retained in the business. They are called 'ploughed-back profits'.
- **Grants:** The government offers finance to firms that are setting up or expanding through the Forbairt agency. At local level the County Enterprise Boards and Leader provide finance.

Note: Sources of finance are also covered in Unit 4.1.

FACTORS INFLUENCING A FIRM'S CHOICE OF FINANCE

- **Cost:** This includes repayments and interest. In times of high interest rates, loans can be an expensive source of finance, whereas the reverse is true in times of low interest rates.
- **Purpose** for which the finance is sought. For example, long-term finance will be used for the purchase of fixed assets, while short-term finance will be used for short-term purposes, e.g. purchase of stocks.

- **Control:** If a firm issues shares to raise finance, it will lose some control to the shareholders, whereas getting a loan will not involve any loss of control.
- **Security:** If the company gets a bank loan, security will have to be provided, but if it issues shares or uses retained earnings, no security is necessary.
- **Tax implications:** Interest payments on loans and hire purchase are tax deductible, whereas dividend payments on shares are not.
- **Gearing:** Debt finance (borrowing) increases a company's gearing, while issuing shares or using retained earnings reduces the gearing. Most firms do not like to be highly geared and as a result try to keep borrowings at a reasonable level.

Working capital management

Working capital is the capital used in the day-to-day running of an enterprise. It is the current assets minus the current liabilities of the company.

Table 5.1: Working capital

Current assets	Current liabilities
• Stocks • Debtors • Cash/bank	• Creditors • Bank overdrafts • Expenses due

Liquidity

This is the relationship between current assets and current liabilities. If current assets are greater than current liabilities, the firm is **liquid.**

Liquidity is measured by the **current ratio** (the ideal is 2:1) and the **acid test ratio** (the ideal is 1:1) (see Unit 4.4).

Proper working capital management

- The firm should be careful about who it gives credit to. It should investigate the **credit history** of the client first.
- Once credit is given, a proper **credit control** policy should be maintained. This involves sending out bills to debtors on time.
- To encourage early payment by debtors, the company should offer cash **discounts**. This is normally in the region of 5 per cent. This will improve cash flow and also reduce the risk of **bad debts**.
- A good **stock control** system will also improve cash flow. If a firm is overstocked, then it has too much cash tied up in stock.
- The firm should delay paying creditors where possible until it has received money from its debtors.
- The firm can draw up **cash flow forecasts** (see Unit 4.1).

- The firm should have a profitable **pricing policy**. The price charged must cover all costs while at the same make a profit for the firm.

OWNERSHIP OPTIONS

- **Sole trader:** A business owned and run by one person or a family. There is no outside control.
- **Partnership:** A business run by two or more people with a view to making a profit.
- **Private limited company:** A business comprising of between one and fifty shareholders. It has a separate legal identity from its owners. The money contributed by the shareholders is called the **share capital**. In return for investing in the business, the shareholders receive a share of company profits, called a **dividend**. They also have a vote at the company AGM. Shareholders have **limited liability**, i.e. in the event of the business failing, they will only lose the amount of their investment; their personal assets cannot be called upon to pay any debts of the business.

Note: All these forms of business ownership are outlined in greater detail in Unit 6.2. A summary chart is included here.

TABLE 5.2: OWNERSHIP OPTIONS

	SOLE TRADER	PARTNERSHIP	PRIVATE LIMITED COMPANY
Formation	Can start immediately if using own name, otherwise must register under Business Names Act.	Can start immediately if using own name, otherwise must register under Business Names Act.	Must send articles and memorandum of association to the Company Registration Office.
Management	Sole trader makes all the decisions.	The partners have an equal say.	Shareholders elect directors to make the decisions.
Liability	Sole trader has unlimited liability.	Partners have unlimited liability.	Shareholders have limited liability.
Legal status	Business is not a separate legal entity from the owner.	Not a separate legal entity from the partners.	The company has a separate legal identity from the owners/shareholders.
Profits	Sole trader keeps all the profits.	Shared equally among the partners.	Some paid out as dividends, the rest retained in business.
Taxation	Sole trader pays PAYE on profits made.	The partnership pays PAYE.	The company pays corporation tax on its profits.

PRODUCTION OPTIONS

Job production

- The product is produced for a specific customer order, e.g. display units for a shop.
- It is not produced for stock. An order will be received before production starts.
- High-level labour skills are needed which require experience and training.
- The product is usually expensive because of the labour costs and quality of materials used.

Batch production

Goods are produced in batches or groups. Examples include the baking of bread, making shoes and clothes of different sizes, printing books, etc.

- Production is not continuous – the batch is produced and production switches to another batch.
- People employed are usually skilled or semi-skilled.
- A certain level of automation is used, which lowers labour costs.
- Goods are produced and held in stock.

Mass production

- This method of production involves non-stop continuous production of the same products, e.g. biscuits in a factory.
- Goods are produced in large quantities and held in stock.
- A high degree of automation is used.
- The majority of the staff would be low- or semi-skilled workers working on assembly-line production.
- These products are generally inexpensive.
- **Economies of scale** usually result from mass production. This means that the cost per unit is reduced as a greater quantity is produced. The reason is that **fixed costs** are spread over a greater production volume.

BUSINESS PLANS

A business plan is a statement issued by the owners or managers of a business outlining how they expect the business to develop over the years ahead.

The business plan should include the following headings: business description, details of owners/management, market analysis, financial analysis, marketing strategies, manufacturing and production and a conclusion.

Business description

- Highlights the background of the business and the products and services it is involved in providing.
- The type of organisation structure will be described here, e.g. sole trader, partnership, limited company.

Details of owners/management

- Contains information about the owners and their backgrounds and experience.
- Details of the management team will be included. The firm's key personnel will be outlined and their positions in the business highlighted.

Market analysis

- This includes details of the size of the market and the firm's share of the total market. The company's **target market** will be identified here.
- Details of competitors will be revealed here. What is their market share and what are their strengths and weaknesses?
- Details of any **market research** undertaken are listed.

Financial analysis

- Outlines sources of finance used by the business, e.g. loan capital, equity finance.
- Past financial records of the firm will be included, e.g. trading and profit and loss accounts and balance sheets for a number of years.
- Future financial projections will be included, e.g. **cash flow forecasts** and projected profit and loss accounts and balance sheets for future years.
- The financing requirements of the firm will be outlined, i.e. how much does the firm need and what for?

Marketing strategies

- Pricing strategies.
- Promotion strategies.
- Distribution strategies.
- Issues relating to the product.

Manufacturing and production

- Details of the equipment and its capacity.
- Details of production methods, e.g. job, batch, mass.
- Details of any quality control systems in place.

Conclusion

A summary of the plan.

Functions/role/importance of a business plan

- Sets out the **goals and objectives** of the firm, both in the short term and the long term, and lays out the strategies that can be used to achieve these goals.
- The plan gives a **focus and direction** to the firm. This will help to **motivate** the management and employees of the business.
- By planning ahead, it may be possible to **foresee future problems** and take action to avoid them.
- The plan can be used as a **benchmark** to compare the actual performance of the business with the targets laid down in the plan.
- The business plan is an important document for the **stakeholders**. It is a source of information for employees, suppliers, shareholders and banks.
- It is a vital document when approaching banks or other investors for **finance** for the business. Lenders/investors will use it to assess the financial viability of the business.

5.4: BUSINESS EXPANSION

Expansion can be achieved from within the business itself or through other businesses outside of itself. Internal growth is referred to as **organic growth**, while growth involving another business is called **inorganic growth**.

REASONS FOR BUSINESS EXPANSION

- **Economies of scale:** By producing larger volumes, a firm's fixed costs are spread over a greater number of units. This means that the cost of producing **each unit** decreases.
- **Diversification:** Many firms do not want to put all their eggs in the one basket. As a result, they may branch out into other lines of business in addition to the main one. This spreads the risk.
- **Safeguard supplies:** If a business is very dependant on certain supplies, then it may make business sense to take over the supplier company in order to guarantee these supplies in the future.
- **Synergy:** This is the theory that if firms merge together, the potential of the two joined firms is greater than the sum of the two enterprises if they remained separate. It is called the '2 + 2 = 5 effect'.
- **Financial strength and security:** A bigger business has greater financial resources and is better able to survive in a competitive marketplace, especially against international competition.

- **Eliminate competition:** If a firm does not grow, competition will. By taking over a rival business, the firm eliminates a threat.
- **Increase product range:** If a firm is looking to add to its product range, it may consider taking over a company with products complimentary to its own.
- **Acquire new skills/technologies:** In order to acquire new skills or technologies, it may make more sense to buy or form a business alliance with a firm that already has them.
- **Esteem needs of owner:** Some business owners simply want their business to be the biggest and to dominate the marketplace. They try to build an empire. This is called 'empire building'.

FINANCE FOR EXPANSION

The finance needed for business expansion is mainly **long-term finance**.

Equity capital

There are two main sources of equity capital:
- **Retained earnings:** These are also called reserves or ploughed-back profits. They are profits made by the business in previous years that have not been spent or paid out as dividends to shareholders. They are retained for the future development of the business.
- **Share capital:** This is finance raised by a company by selling shares (part-ownership) in the business to anyone who is willing to invest. In return for buying shares, the shareholders get a part-ownership of the business and a share of the profits every year, called a dividend.

Benefits of using equity capital for expansion
- It is a cheap source of finance since no interest has to be paid and the money does not have to be paid back.
- The company does not have to provide security to raise the capital. If getting a bank loan, fixed assets must be provided as security.
- Equity finance puts less financial pressure on a firm than a loan. Loans increase the firm's gearing, whereas equity capital reduces it.

Drawbacks of equity (share) capital
- When shares are sold to raise finance, the control of the existing shareholders is reduced.
- The payment of dividends is not a tax-deductible expense for the company, whereas the repayment of interest on a loan is.
- Share issues can be very expensive, especially for large companies listed on the stock exchange.

Loan capital

The alternative to funding an expansion with equity capital is to borrow money from the bank.

Benefits of using loan capital for expansion
- In times of low interest rates, this can be a cheap source of finance, and there are none of the expenses of issuing shares.
- Although security has to be provided, there is no direct loss of control in the business.
- Interest payments on loans are tax deductible, which helps to reduce the cost of the loan.
- Loan repayments and interest can be tailored to suit the cash flow of the business.

Drawbacks of loan capital
- Repayments plus interest must be made regardless of profit levels. This puts financial pressure on the company.
- Loans increase the firm's gearing, which will make it more difficult to attract shareholders in the future.
- Security has to be provided for loans. This is usually in the form of fixed assets.

METHODS OF EXPANSION

Business expansion can be divided into organic and inorganic growth.

Organic growth

Organic growth is the growth of the business from within. It is the natural growth of the firm and involves increasing sales, either at home and/or internationally.
- **Increasing sales domestically:** The firm attempts to increase sales by promoting and advertising its goods. This may involve opening new branches.
- **Exporting:** If the domestic market is small, the firm may look to international markets in order to increase its sales. As a member of the EU, Ireland can trade freely with other EU countries.
- **Franchising:** Instead of opening up new branches of the business themselves, management may decide to franchise out the name. This allows another person to open a branch of the firm in exchange for a fee and a percentage of sales (see Unit 6.2).
- **New products/services**: The firm may add to the range of products/services it provides, e.g. as part of Aer Lingus's expansion programme, it started long-haul flights to Dubai in 2006.

Inorganic growth

Inorganic growth is the expansion of the firm with the involvement of an outside company. Inorganic growth is a quicker growth strategy than organic growth.

Acquisition/takeover

This is where one company gets control of another by buying a majority of the voting share capital. Examples of takeovers include Eircom's purchase of Meteor for €420 million and the takeover of National Irish Bank by the Danish bank Danske Bank. The main benefit of a takeover is that it allows growth to take place quickly by instantly increasing the customer base.

Alliance/joint venture

This is a partnership agreement between two firms for the mutual benefit of both. The businesses may agree to come together to share technology, help market each other's products/services or help with distribution. However, both firms remain separate entities. An example of an alliance is SuperValu and Lynch Hotels.

Benefits of alliances include the following.
- Both parties benefit through shared skills, marketing and sales, etc.
- The alliance is a voluntary, temporary arrangement and so can be easily ended.
- It increases the range of services that each firm has to offer, which should make both businesses more competitive.

Merger

A merger is when two businesses join together to become one. This is usually a permanent move that is agreed between both firms. An example of a merger is the Irish packaging firm Smurfit, which merged with the Dutch packaging firm Kappa in 2006 to form Smurfit Kappa, the largest packaging firm in Europe. This will allow cost savings to be made due to economies of scale and provide security and financial strength for the new operation.

Implications of expansion

The implications of expansion will be both short and long term.
- **Profits:** In the long run, the organisation's profits will increase. This will mainly be due to entering new markets and savings as a result of economies of scale.
- **Organisational structure:** When firms expand, they usually need to change their structure. The functional (line) structure may have to be changed to a product structure.

- **Financial structure:** An expansion will require a lot of additional finance. Many mergers and takeovers are now financed by debt. As a result, the gearing of the company will increase.
- **Redundancies:** A rationalisation programme to cut costs usually follows a takeover or merger. This involves redundancies.
- **Consumers:** A bigger firm may lose the personal touch that it had before the expansion.

Importance of Irish business expansion in domestic markets

- Bigger businesses have a greater chance of **survival** in the marketplace. This is often because they are involved in exporting and are less dependent on the domestic markets.
- Large firms employ more people and make more profits. As a result, they contribute large amounts of **tax revenue**, like income taxes and corporation taxes, to the government.
- Large companies tend to export more goods and services. This leads to an improvement in Ireland's **balance of trade** and **balance of payments**.
- By expanding, firms create **employment**, which reduces unemployment levels.
- Larger companies have more money to invest in **research and development**. This improves the quality of products and services and makes these firms **competitive** with large multinationals.

Importance of Irish business expansion into foreign markets

- Irish firms that set up abroad **repatriate** some or all of their **profits** back to Ireland. This increases the wealth in Ireland.
- By expanding into foreign markets, Irish firms come into contact with **new technologies and skills** that can be brought back and used in Ireland.
- Irish firms that expand abroad increase the **profile** of Irish business and Ireland as a country. For example, Kerry Group is known around the world. This helps to attract business to Ireland.
- The Irish market is too small to sustain large-scale expansion. Therefore, to achieve real **economies of scale** and become internationally competitive, Irish businesses must expand into foreign markets.

EXAM QUESTIONS

Exam question 1

Contrast equity and loan capital as sources of finance for expansion. (30 marks)

Marking scheme

Five points of contrast are needed here at **6 marks** each. The 6 marks are split into **2 marks** for naming the point of contrast, **2 marks** for applying it to equity finance and **2 marks** for applying it to loan finance.

Sample answer

- **Cost (2 marks):** Equity (share) capital is a cheap source of finance since it does not have to be repaid. **(2 marks)** Loan capital, on the other hand, has to be repaid with interest. **(2 marks)**
- **Security (2 marks):** No security has to be provided when a company raises share capital **(2 marks)**, whereas if the firm gets a loan, it has to provide fixed assets as security. **(2 marks)**
- **Control (2 marks):** By issuing shares, the owners of the business are losing some of their control over the company, as the new shareholders now have a part-ownership. **(2 marks)** There is no loss of control if the expansion is funded with loan capital. **(2 marks)**
- **Gearing (2 marks):** Getting a loan to finance expansion increases the gearing of the company. **(2 marks)** Selling shares, on the other hand, reduces the gearing of the firm. **(2 marks)**
- **Tax implications (2 marks):** Interest payments on loans are tax deductible, which can reduce the cost of borrowing. **(2 marks)** Dividends paid to shareholders are not tax deductible. **(2 marks)**

IMPORTANT DEFINITIONS FROM UNIT 5

- **Feasibility study:** A study carried out on a new product/service to assess if it would be both commercially and technically viable.
- **Prototype:** A first working model of a product from which subsequent copies are made or improved specimens developed. It proves that the product can be made.
- **Test marketing:** Testing the reaction of a small group of people to a product or service before going into full production.
- **Market research:** This is the collecting, recording and detailed examination of all data relating to the transfer of goods from the producer to the consumer.
- **Marketing concept:** This involves identifying and satisfying consumer needs profitably. The firm puts the customer first at all times.
- **Market segmentation:** Different consumers have different needs and wants from products and services. As a result, companies break the market up into segments to satisfy these different needs. This is also called target marketing.
- **Marketing mix:** The four Ps of marketing: product, price, promotion and place.
- **Branding:** The marking of goods with a clearly identifiable name, mark or symbol. The aim is to give the product its own identity.
- **Product life cycle:** The stages that all products go through: introduction, growth, maturity, saturation and decline.
- **Sales promotion:** All means of promoting goods or services other than direct advertising. They include money off, buy one get one free, 50 per cent extra free, etc.
- **Public relations:** This involves all attempts by the company to create and maintain a good public image for the firm, e.g. sponsorship.
- **Channels of distribution:** The means by which goods get from the producer to the consumer. Channels include the wholesaler, retailer and agent.
- **Liquidity:** The firm's ability to pay its short-term debts as they fall due. Liquidity is measured by the current ratio and the acid test ratio.
- **Working capital management:** Working capital is current assets minus current liabilities. The management of it involves stock control, credit control and cash flow forecasts.
- **Limited liability:** In the event of a company failing, the shareholders only lose their investment in it. Their personal assets cannot be called on to pay company debts.
- **Business plan:** A document drawn up by the owners of a business outlining how they expect the business to develop in the years ahead.
- **Equity finance:** The internal capital of the firm. It includes the share capital and retained earnings (reserves).
- **Alliance:** A partnership agreement between two firms for the mutual benefit of both. However, both firms remain separate entities.
- **Merger:** Two businesses join together to become one. This is a permanent move agreed by both firms, e.g. Kappa and Smurfit.

CHAPTER 6
Unit 6: Domestic Environment

There are three categories of industry: primary, secondary and tertiary (services).

PRIMARY INDUSTRIES

Agriculture

The number of people involved in farming has been in decline for many years now.

- Small farms are no longer viable to run. As a result, small farmers have been selling out to bigger farmers and getting out of the business.
- Disease and health scares in recent years, such as foot and mouth disease, BSE and bird flu, have had an adverse affect on farming.
- Reforms of the Common Agricultural Policy (CAP) have removed many of the subsidies paid to farmers. From 2005, farmers get a single EU payment, which will eventually be phased out. This means that only the most efficient farmers will survive.

Fishing

The fishing industry in Ireland is small and is centred on a small number of fishing ports around the country, e.g. Killybegs, Dunmore East and Kilmore Quay. The EU Common Fisheries Policy controls fishing in EU states. This puts a limit on the amount of fish that can be caught in EU waters. Employment in this sector is small.

Mining

Ireland's mining industry is small. A large gas reserve off the coast of Kinsale supplies much of the country with natural gas through a pipeline network. There are also mines at Galmoy in Kilkenny and Navan in Meath. Employment in the sector is small.

Forestry

The forestry industry is run by the state agency, Coillte. The government provides grants for the planting of trees in order to develop the industry in Ireland. Farmers are also being encouraged to plant marginal land as an alternative to farming it.

Trends in the primary sector

- Employment in agriculture is declining due to small farms becoming less viable to run. Small farmers are getting out of farming.
- There have been changes in the nature of farming. Organic farm produce is becoming increasingly popular with consumers due to health scares with traditional farm produce.
- Employment in the fishing industry is declining, as EU regulations have put limits on the number of days per month fishermen can fish.

SECONDARY SECTOR: MANUFACTURING/CONSTRUCTION

Indigenous firms

These are firms that are set up, owned and run by Irish people.

Benefits of indigenous firms:
- They have a loyalty to the area and the country.
- They provide employment in the local area.
- They help other businesses in the area by buying raw materials and services from them, which creates spin-off business.
- They reinvest their profits in Ireland.

Transnationals

Transnationals are firms with headquarters in one country and branches in many other countries. Examples include Sony, Shell, Coca Cola and Microsoft. IDA Ireland (the Industrial Development Authority) is responsible for attracting such companies to Ireland.

Note: Transnational companies are discussed in more detail in Unit 6.2.

Agribusiness

These are firms that are in some way connected with agriculture. They include all types of food production firms as well as all firms involved in producing supplies or equipment to farmers. Examples include Glanbia, Kerry Group and Golden Vale. This is an important sector in the Irish economy and produces output for both the Irish and export markets. Manufacturers in the agribusiness sector face tough competition from foreign firms due to the open nature of the EU market.

Construction

This industry provides a lot of employment. Most construction firms are indigenous, which results in their profits being retained in Ireland.

Trends in the secondary sector

- Many of the traditional indigenous manufacturing firms have closed due to competition from low-wage economies. Employment has fallen dramatically as a result.
- A growing number of firms, both indigenous and foreign owned, have set up in the technology and electronics sector, e.g. Intel is a big employer in Co. Kildare.
- Due to intense competition in the agribusiness sector, some firms have merged in order to achieve economies of scale, e.g. Avonmore and Waterford Foods became Glanbia.

TERTIARY SECTOR: SERVICE INDUSTRIES

This is the fastest-growing sector in the economy. Examples of service industries include banking, insurance, transport, tourism and leisure, catering, retailing, communications, professional services and public sector employment.

Reasons for the growth of the tertiary sector

- Due to the Celtic Tiger, Irish people have a higher standard of living and more disposable income to spend on services, e.g. many families now take two holidays a year.
- Due to inward migration of returning Irish people and an influx of non-nationals, Ireland's population is currently at its highest since the Famine. This has led to a huge increase in the demand for services.
- In many families, both parents are now working outside the home. This has led to a greater demand for child care services.
- Service sector growth has been driven by the growth of the ICT sector. It is vital for businesses to have up-to-date technology.
- Longer life expectancy due to better medical care has in turn led to further need for medical and health care facilities for the elderly.

Exam Tip: The reasons for the growth of the tertiary sector are the same as the trends in the sector.

The importance of the tertiary sector to the economy

- Between 60 and 70 per cent of the Irish labour force is employed in the tertiary sector.
- More than 80 per cent of small businesses in Ireland are in the services sector. This contributes huge amounts of tax revenue to the government, e.g. PAYE of workers, VAT and corporation tax.
- Irish service companies now deal in export markets as well as the home market. For example, Irish firms can now tender for contracts in other EU countries.

6.2: TYPES OF BUSINESS ORGANISATION

The following types of business organisations will be discussed:
- Sole trader.
- Partnership.
- Private limited company.
- Public limited company.
- Alliances.
- Franchising.
- Co-operatives.
- Transnationals.
- State-owned enterprises.
- Indigenous firms.

Exam Tip: You should know the following for each of these types of business organisation:
- Definition.
- Formation.
- Characteristics.
- Advantages and disadvantages.

SOLE TRADER

This is a business owned and run by one person, e.g. grocer, hairdresser, publican.

Formation

If the sole trader trades under his own name, he may start immediately, e.g. Wilson's Wine Bar. If he is using a name different to his own, e.g. The Vineyard, then he must register the business under the Business Names Act 1963.

Advantages and disadvantages of being a sole trader

ADVANTAGES	DISADVANTAGES
• Keeps all the profits. • Own boss – makes all the decisions. • Does not have to publish accounts. • Easy to set up.	• Suffers all the losses. • Has unlimited liability. • Difficulty in raising finance for expansion. • May have to work long hours.

PARTNERSHIP

A partnership is the relationship that exists between two and twenty people with a view to making a profit.

Formation

If the partners operate under their own names, the partnership can start immediately. Otherwise it must be registered under the Business Names Act 1963. The partners will usually draw up their own rules. This is called a deed of partnership.

Advantages and disadvantages of partnerships

ADVANTAGES	DISADVANTAGES
• Easier to raise capital with more owners. • Different skills and talents are available. • Losses are shared equally among the partners. • Accounts do not have to be published.	• Partners have unlimited liability. • Partnership must be dissolved on the death of a partner. • Disagreements may arise between the partners.

PRIVATE LIMITED COMPANY (LTD)

A private limited company is a business owned by between one and fifty shareholders, which has a separate legal identity in the eyes of the law.

Formation

A number of documents have to be sent to the Registrar of Companies:

- **Memorandum of association:** This document is a summary of what the company was set up to do. It outlines the relationship between the company and the public. It contains:
  - ➤ The name and address of the company.
  - ➤ The objectives for which the company was set up.
  - ➤ The amount of authorised share capital.
  - ➤ A statement that the shareholders have limited liability.
- **Articles of association:** This document sets out the internal rules and regulations of the company. It contains:
  - ➤ Details of share capital and voting rights attaching to shares.
  - ➤ Details of how meetings are to be called and conducted.
  - ➤ Details of how the directors are to be elected and duties of the directors.
  - ➤ How the company can be wound up (closed down).
- **Form A1:** This form contains:
  - ➤ Amount of authorised and issued share capital.
  - ➤ List of those who have agreed to become directors.
  - ➤ Declaration of compliance with the Companies Acts.
- These documents are all then sent to the **Registrar of Companies.** If everything is in order, the Registrar will issue a **certificate of incorporation** for the company. This is the 'birth certificate' of the company and recognises that it now legally exists. Incorporation means:
  - ➤ The company has a separate legal identity from its owners. It can sue and be sued in its own name.
  - ➤ The shareholders have limited liability.
  - ➤ The company has continuity of existence.
  - ➤ The new company must now hold a **statutory meeting** before starting to trade.

Characteristics

- Between one and fifty shareholders.
- The last name must be Limited (Ltd).
- Shares are not bought and sold by members of the public.
- Private limited companies are often family affairs.

Advantages and disadvantages of private limited companies

ADVANTAGES	DISADVANTAGES
<ul><li>With up to 50 shareholders, it is easy to raise finance for expansion.</li><li>The shareholders have limited liability.</li><li>The company has a separate legal identity from its owners. The firm must be sued, not the owners.</li><li>Generally, companies have better credit ratings than sole traders or partnerships.</li></ul>	<ul><li>There are many formalities and expenses involved in setting up.</li><li>There may be conflicts between the shareholders and the directors if they are not the same people.</li><li>The annual accounts must be sent to the Registrar of Companies.</li><li>Shares cannot be sold to the general public, which restricts access to capital.</li></ul>

PUBLIC LIMITED COMPANY (PLC)

This is a business with at least seven shareholders and no maximum, in which shares are bought and sold freely on the stock exchange.

Formation

Before trading, in addition to getting a certificate of incorporation, a public limited company must get a **trading certificate** from the Registrar of Companies.

Characteristics

- At least seven shareholders and no maximum.
- The letters PLC must appear after the name.
- Shares are bought and sold freely on the stock exchange by whoever wants to buy them.
- Examples of PLCs are AIB, Bank of Ireland, Glanbia, Kerry Group and Ryanair.

Advantages and disadvantages of public limited companies

ADVANTAGES	DISADVANTAGES
• Can raise a lot of capital as a result of being listed on the stock exchange. • There is free publicity with being quoted on the stock exchange. • Public companies can attract top management. • Free/cheap shares can be given to management and employees, which motivates them to work hard. • Public companies can use their shares as part payment in any takeovers.	• Setting up PLCs is very expensive and involves a lot of legal formality. • Public companies are subject to much legal regulation. These include stock exchange rules and the Companies Acts. • Detailed accounts have to be published each year, which means that competitors have sensitive information on the company. • Since PLCs' shares are quoted on the stock exchange, the company may become the target of a takeover bid.

ALLIANCE

An alliance is a partnership agreement between two firms for the mutual benefit of both. The businesses agree to come together to share skills or resources.

Formation

An alliance is formed when two firms decide that it would be beneficial for both of them to join up for some activity on a temporary basis.

Characteristics

- The firms join up for a specific purpose to improve the performance of both in the marketplace. An alliance may be formed for the purposes of marketing, distribution or product development.
- Both firms retain their own identities.
- The alliance may be short or long term.
- An alliance may also be called a joint venture. An example of an alliance is An Post and the Belgian bank Fortis.

Advantages and disadvantages of alliances

ADVANTAGES	DISADVANTAGES
• Both firms benefit from the skills and expertise of the other without the costs of acquiring these skills. • An alliance may allow the joint enterprise to achieve economies of scale and help them to survive. • Both firms have a recognised brand name which will help the other. • Expensive new product development costs can be shared.	• Disagreements may arise about the exact role of both firms in the alliance. • Customers may feel that their choice is restricted as each firm promotes the products of the other. • If one firm performs badly, it may have a negative impact on the other's reputation.

FRANCHISE

A franchise is when an established business allows another business to set up and use its name in exchange for a fee and a percentage of the sales.

Formation

The franchiser is an expanding business and wants to open new branches but does not want to manage these branches. She seeks out an interested party (franchisee) and charges a fee for the use of the business name.

Characteristics

- This is a means of business expansion for the franchiser, which involves other people (franchisees) opening new branches under the original business name.
- The franchisee pays a fee to the franchiser and then a percentage of the sales revenue each year.
- Each new branch contains the same standard décor, product range, pricing strategy, etc.
- Examples of franchises are Supermacs, O'Brien's Sandwich Bars and Godfathers Pizzas.

Advantages and disadvantages of franchises

ADVANTAGES	DISADVANTAGES
• The franchiser can open new branches without major expense, as the franchisee pays an initial fee. • Due to an already established name, the risk of failure is small. • The business benefits from national advertising and promotion. • The franchisee is guaranteed that there will be no other branches opening in the same area. • Economies of scale result from bulk buying of stocks.	• The franchiser is taking a risk of the franchisee not running the business properly and perhaps damaging the group's reputation. • The costs to the franchisee are high. An initial fee must be paid and then an annual percentage of the sales. • There is not much room for the franchisee to be creative, as a standard formula must be followed.

CO-OPERATIVE

A co-operative is a business set up by a group of people with a common need. Each member has an equal say in the running of the business.

Formation

The members (a minimum of seven) draw up the rules (similar to the memorandum and articles of association) of the co-op and send them to the Registrar of Friendly Societies. If these are in order, a certificate of registration is issued and the co-op can begin trading.

Characteristics

● Co-ops are regulated by the Industrial and Provident Societies Acts 1893–1978.
● Co-ops are democratically run, i.e. each member has one vote regardless of the number of shares held.
● Profits are distributed to the members based on the proportion of business they do with the co-op.
● Examples of co-ops are agricultural co-ops and credit unions.

Advantages and disadvantages of co-operatives

ADVANTAGES	DISADVANTAGES
• Democratically run; each member has an equal say in the running of the co-op, regardless of the number of shares held. • The members have limited liability. • Co-ops have good credit ratings with banks and can borrow quite easily. • Members share profits in proportion to the volume of business done with the co-op.	• The formation and running of the co-op is subject to a lot of regulation. • It may be difficult to attract new members due to the common bond that must exist. This may limit the amount of capital that can be raised. • Conflicts may arise between owners and the management committee elected to run the co-op.

TRANSNATIONALS

A transnational/multinational is a company with its headquarters in one country and branches in many other countries. They are also called multinationals.

Formation

Firms become transnationals due to growth and expansion of the business.

Characteristics

- They tend to be the largest companies in the world. Examples include Sony, Shell, Coca Cola, Microsoft and McDonald's.
- They sell standardised products all over the world, sometimes with slight modifications to suit different countries.
- Transnationals practically control world trade.

Ireland and transnationals

The Industrial Development Authority (IDA) attracts foreign companies to set up in Ireland. Examples include Intel, Hewlett Packard, Google (European HQ in Dublin), Amazon and eBay. Reasons why they choose Ireland:
- **Tax concessions:** Ireland offers a 12.5 per cent corporation tax rate (the tax that companies pay on their profits).

- **Access to the EU market:** By setting up in Ireland, transnationals have access to the huge EU market.
- **Educated workforce:** Ireland has one of the best-educated workforces in the world.
- **Grants:** The IDA offers attractive grants to firms that set up here.
- **Stable currency:** Being part of the euro currency reduces exchange rate risks for firms that set up in Ireland.

Advantages and disadvantages of transnationals

ADVANTAGES (TO IRELAND)	DISADVANTAGES (TO IRELAND)
• Transnationals employ almost 150,000 people in Ireland. • A huge amount of tax revenue is generated, including PAYE, VAT and corporation tax. • TNCs export most of their output, which improves Ireland's balance of trade and balance of payments. • Many Irish firms prosper as a result of spin-off business created from TNCs. • TNCs bring a high level of skills and management expertise to Ireland.	• TNCs have no real loyalty to Ireland. If they can operate cheaper elsewhere, then they will leave, which causes unemployment. • TNCs repatriate their profits back to their home country. • They provide intense competition to Irish firms. This may result in the closure of some Irish firms. • Sometimes they can have a negative effect on the environment.

STATE-OWNED ENTERPRISES

State-owned enterprises are companies set up, owned and managed by the government. They are also known as state-sponsored bodies or semi-state companies.

Formation

These companies are usually set up by an Act of the Oireachtas or they may be set up as limited companies with the government as the major shareholder.

Characteristics

- Some of the biggest businesses in Ireland are owned by the government, e.g. RTÉ, An Post, Dublin Bus.

- Each state company is under the control of a government minister, who appoints a board of directors to run the company.
- State firms are both commercial and non-commercial. For example, An Post and RTÉ charge for their services, while Fáilte Ireland does not.

Advantages and disadvantages of state-owned enterprises

ADVANTAGES	DISADVANTAGES
• State-owned firms provide a lot of employment. There are 35,000 people employed in state-owned firms. • State-owned firms provide essential services in non-profit areas, e.g. ESB, An Post. • Economic development is promoted through state firms, e.g. IDA Ireland. • State-owned firms develop the natural resources of the country, e.g. Bord Gáis.	• Some semi-state companies are inefficient and overstaffed. This may result in higher prices for consumers. • Some of these firms make losses, which are paid for by the taxpayer. • The European Commission has outlawed state aid to semi-state companies. This may make it difficult for them to survive. • Sometimes management positions may be politically influenced.

INDIGENOUS FIRMS

Indigenous firms are firms set up, owned and run by Irish people.

Characteristics

- The government supports the creation of indigenous firms through Enterprise Ireland. The aim is to lessen our dependence on multinationals.
- Enterprise Ireland gives grants, advice and start-up finance to indigenous firms.

Note: Benefits of indigenous firms are covered in Unit 6.1

Exam Tip: Almost every year, students are asked to compare/contrast two different types of business organisation. In some cases, using a set of common themes can achieve this. However, sometimes it is easier to just write a paragraph on each type of business given.

Changing trends in ownership and structure

- There has been an increase in the number of **franchises** in Ireland. A franchise is an organic method of expansion.
- More firms are entering into **mergers and alliances**, as they see this as a means of sharing expertise and cutting costs, e.g. Smurfit's merger with Kappa.
- There has been a trend towards **privatisation** of state firms. Telecom Éireann became Eircom in 1999 and Aer Lingus was privatised in 2006.
- Some larger companies, including co-ops, have changed their structures to **PLCs**, e.g. Kerry Group, Golden Vale.
- Many sole traders and partnerships have converted to **private limited companies** because of the benefits of limited liability.
- Some of the larger Irish firms have expanded to become **transnationals** by making acquisitions abroad, e.g. CRH and Kerry Group.

Reasons for changing trends in ownership and structure

- **Growth:** As firms grow, the structure that they started off with may no longer allow for further expansion. For example, a sole trader may need more expertise and skills that will be easier to acquire if they change to a company status.
- **Limited liability:** In order to reduce personal risk, a sole trader or partnership may convert to a private limited company.
- **Capital:** A private limited company may convert to PLC status in order to raise large amounts of capital on the stock exchange.
- **Marketing:** Firms enter into alliances or form mergers to increase the marketing appeal of both, e.g. SuperValu and Lynch Hotels.
- **New skills and expertise:** A change in structure will enable a firm to attract new management with new skills and expertise. For example, a PLC has a better chance of attracting top management than a private limited company.
- **Economies of scale:** As firms produce on a larger scale, it becomes cheaper to produce each unit. PLC status allows firms to grow large enough to achieve economies of scale.

EXAM QUESTIONS

Exam question 1

Contrast a private limited company with a public limited company as a form of business organisation. (20 marks)

Marking scheme
Four points of contrast at **5 marks** each. The 5 marks is split into **1 mark** for naming the point of contrast, **2 marks** for applying it to a private company and **2 marks** for applying it to a public company.

Sample answer
The easiest way to answer this question is in a tabular format, since the points of contrast can be applied to both.

	PRIVATE COMPANY	PUBLIC COMPANY
Formation (1 mark)	Can start trading upon receipt of a certificate of incorporation. (**2 marks**)	Needs a trading certificate in addition to a certificate of incorporation. (**2 marks**)
Ownership (1 mark)	Between one and fifty shareholders. (**2 marks**)	Minimum seven shareholders; no maximum. (**2 marks**)
Accounts (1 mark)	Do not have to be published. (**2 marks**)	Have to be published. (**2 marks**)
Finance (1 mark)	More difficulty raising finance since not listed on the stock exchange. (**2 marks**)	Easier to raise finance since listed on the stock exchange. (**2 marks**)

Exam question 2

Contrast an alliance and a franchise as forms of business organisation. Use examples in your answer. (30 marks)

Marking scheme

15 marks for each type of organisation. Two pieces of information on each at **5 marks** and two examples at **5 marks** each.

Sample answer

In this case, the two types of business organisation given are completely different and cannot really be contrasted under a set of common points. The best approach here is to write a paragraph on each for **15 marks,** split as in exam question 1.

6.3: COMMUNITY DEVELOPMENT

Community development means reviving and developing local areas and communities by encouraging local community initiatives and the development of locally owned and run businesses.

REASONS FOR LOCAL COMMUNITY DEVELOPMENT

- **Indigenous firms** will have a sense of loyalty to the area, which will reduce the dependence on foreign multinationals.
- These local firms that set up will purchase goods and services from other local companies. This is called **spin-off** business.
- By encouraging business to locate in local communities, the problem of **unemployment** is tackled.
- As businesses set up in local communities, an **enterprise culture** is created in the area, which means that a feeling of **entrepreneurship** and self-confidence develops.
- In order to develop the **infrastructure** in the locality, a community needs local business.

HOW THE LOCAL COMMUNITY BENEFITS FROM LOCAL BUSINESS

- **Direct and indirect employment** is created. Locals will be employed directly in the business and others will be employed in spin-off business that will be created.

- There will be **wealth creation** in the local area. Local firms will bring employment and wealth to the area. As a result, people's **standard of living** will improve.
- An **enterprise culture** will be created in the area. The success of local business will have a knock-on effect on others who may start their own business.
- The local community gets a **sense of security** from having local businesses in the area as opposed to foreign firms that are not committed to the locality. Future development can be planned.
- The **infrastructure** will be improved in the community since new business will require it. Roads, broadband internet connections, public services, etc. will get more funding.

COMMUNITY DEVELOPMENT INCORPORATING LOCAL COMMUNITY INITIATIVES

LEADER Plus

This is an EU community initiative for **rural** development.

Provisions, services, benefits and role
- LEADER is the EU community initiative to help **rural development**.
- Projects should be **innovative** and have the potential to act as a model for other areas, i.e. be transferable.
- **Grants** are given by LEADER to fund local projects that fit the criteria. Up to 50 per cent of the cost of the project is funded.
- Grants are also given for local groups to carry out **feasibility studies** in the area.
- LEADER has an aim of **creating jobs** and reducing unemployment. Training and recruitment assistance is given.
- **Local tourism and craft enterprises** are promoted and encouraged.
- **Aim:** Projects based locally mean locals have a sense of ownership of them and are more committed to them.

County Enterprise Boards

County Enterprise Boards (CEBs) are local government agencies that help entrepreneurs start up small businesses and create employment in their own county.

- The **aim** is to help small local businesses, generally with less than ten employees, to set up and survive.
- They have access to a **county enterprise fund** from government, which is used to help entrepreneurs set up small businesses.

- They draw up **county enterprise action plans**, which examine a county's strengths and weaknesses and make proposals for job creation.
- They give **grants** to entrepreneurs to set up. These fund feasibility studies and up to 50 per cent of the cost of fixed assets.
- They help **create local employment** by developing small firms with generally less than ten employees. **Training** in all aspects of the business is provided.
- Each CEB provides **mentors**. These are experienced businesspeople who will guide and give **advice** to the new firms during their early stages.
- The CEB will provide **advice** to the new ventures in areas such as market research, finance and management.
- Projects must be **commercially and economically viable**, i.e. be able to stand on their own feet within two years.

FÁS schemes

FÁS is the state training and employment agency. It runs a number of schemes to advise and train workers and to help unemployed people get work.

Community Enterprise Programme

- **Trains** people in the local area.
- Gives **advice** to people who are starting their own business.
- Helps with **recruitment and selection** of staff.
- Gives grants for the preparation of **business plans** and **feasibility studies**.

Area Partnership Companies (APC)

They operate mainly in disadvantaged inner cities. Each APC tries to serve the specific needs of its own area. The aim is to create more jobs at local level, particularly for the long-term unemployed in disadvantaged areas.

Exam Tip: Students are usually allowed to select and write about the community agency **of choice**. However, they may be asked about a certain agency.

Exam Tip: If a question asks about a community development organisation **in your locality**, then be sure to give local examples. They can be any examples from the local area.

EXAM QUESTIONS

Exam question 1

Community development organisations are set up to help local business enterprises. Describe the services provided by one community development organisation. (20 marks)

Marking scheme

Four points at **5 marks** each. The 5 marks are split into **2 marks** for naming the point and **3 marks** for a short development of it.

Sample answer

The organisation chosen is the County Enterprise Board (CEB).

- **Advice (2 marks):** The CEB gives advice to new enterprises in areas such as marketing, management, finance, etc. A CEB official meets with the business owner. **(3 marks)**
- **Grants (2 marks):** The CEB provides grants for the purchase of fixed assets (up to 50 per cent) and also for the new business to carry out a feasibility study. **(3 marks)**
- **Mentoring service (2 marks):** Experienced businesspeople, called mentors, are assigned to each new business enterprise to give advice and guidance in the early stages. **(3 marks)**
- **Training (2 marks):** New business owners are trained in areas such as staffing, marketing and customer service. Guest speakers are brought in to talk to the owners. **(3 marks)**

6.4: BUSINESS AND THE ECONOMY

The four **factors of production** are land, labour, capital and enterprise.

THE IMPACT OF THE ECONOMY ON BUSINESS (ECONOMIC VARIABLES)

The economy has an impact on business through items called **economic variables**. Economic variables are inflation, interest rates, exchange rates, taxation, grants and subsidies and unemployment.

Inflation

Inflation is an increase in the cost of living from one year to the next. It is measured by the Consumer Price Index (CPI).

Low rates of inflation are better for business and the economy in general.

- If inflation is low, then **prices of goods and services** to the Irish consumer are stable. This means that firms will produce and sell more, which increases profits. High inflation rates will lead to reduced purchasing by consumers, which will reduce firms' **sales and profits**.
- If inflation is low, Irish firms will be more competitive when trading abroad, which will have a positive impact on our **balance of trade** and **balance of payments**. If it is high, then Irish firms will be less competitive abroad.
- Low inflation rates mean Irish manufacturers will buy their **raw materials** in Ireland rather than look abroad. High inflation may force them to buy abroad.
- High inflation may result in unions looking for **wage increases**. This may cause industrial action. Low inflation rates help to maintain a stable **industrial relations** climate.

Interest rates

Interest rates represent the cost of money borrowed or the return on money saved.

The European Central Bank (ECB) now sets interest rates for the Eurozone.

- Low interest rates result in **consumer borrowing** and spending, which leads to an increased demand for goods and services. This in turn increases sales and profits of business. High interest rates have the opposite effect and are bad for business.
- When interest rates are low, firms can borrow more money to **expand** their business. This results in them becoming more **competitive** in domestic and international markets. High interest rates have the opposite effect.
- High interest rates are also negative for business because **investors** may put their money into deposit accounts in banks rather than buy shares in companies. Thus, business may have difficulty **raising finance** from share issues.
- For firms with reserves (savings), high interest rates are good.

Exchange rates

The exchange rate is the value at which one currency can be exchanged for another.

- Exchange rates affect firms that trade internationally (they are not relevant when trading with other Eurozone countries). However, Ireland does a lot of trade with the US and the UK, and as a result, exchange rates are very important to us.

- Our main trading partner is the UK, so the most important exchange rate is the euro/sterling rate.
- A strong euro in relation to other currencies (high exchange rate) is bad for exporters, as it means the currency received for the exports converts to less euro. For example, compare €1 = £0.68 sterling and €1 = £0.72 sterling. Suppose an Irish exporter makes a price with an English buyer for a consignment of goods (to be delivered in three months' time) at £340,000 sterling at an exchange rate of €1 = £0.68. This converts to €500,000 (£340,000 ÷ £0.68) that the Irish exporter hopes to receive. Suppose at the time of delivery and payment the rate has changed to €1 = £0.72. The Irish exporter gets the £340,000, as agreed. However, this now converts to €472,222 (£340,000 ÷ £0.72), which is substantially less than the expected €500,000. The exporter's profit suffers as a result.
- A strong euro is good for importers, as it means foreign currency can be purchased more cheaply to pay for the imports.
- A weak euro in relation to other currencies (low exchange rate) is good for exporters, as it means that Irish goods are cheap when priced in other currencies. This makes them easier to sell and increases sales and profits of exporting firms.
- A weak euro is bad for importers.
- Due to exchange rates between the euro and other currencies **fluctuating**, there is **uncertainty** for firms that are involved in foreign trade. A price set at today's rate may not be worth the same as when payment takes place due to the exchange rate changing in the meantime. This may affect profits of the exporter/importer.

Taxation

Taxes are compulsory payments made to the government. The main business taxes are income tax, corporation tax, VAT, motor tax and possibly capital taxes.

Lower rates of tax are better for business.
- **PAYE:** The tax workers pay on their wages. The two rates of income tax in force as of 2006 are 20 per cent and 42 per cent. If these rates are kept low, then workers have more money to spend, which results in firms selling more. Thus, they make more profits. Also, if rates are lower, workers are happier to work and industrial relations problems are less likely to occur.
- **Corporation tax:** The tax that companies pay on their profits. As of 2006, the rate is 12.5 per cent. Lower corporation tax results in firms having more retained profits, which they can then plough back into the business to finance expansion and help them become more competitive with foreign firms.
- **VAT:** Low VAT rates mean lower prices and more goods and services purchased by consumers. This leads to increased sales and profits for companies and keeps them competitive.

Grants and subsidies

Grants are non-repayable sums of money given to businesses by the government to help them start up or expand.

Subsidies are payments by the government to certain businesses or industries. They are normally a form of price support.

- Both indigenous and foreign firms are given grants. IDA Ireland gives grants to foreign companies to locate in Ireland. Enterprise Ireland helps indigenous Irish firms.
- Grants are also given to firms to locate in certain areas, e.g. Gaeltacht regions.
- At local level, each county has a County Enterprise Board, which gives grants to indigenous firms starting up in the local area.

Unemployment

Unemployment refers to the number of people who are available and looking for work but who cannot get a job.

- High unemployment means less money being spent in the economy, which reduces sales and profits for businesses.
- In addition, high unemployment means more social welfare payments, which may mean increased taxes have to be charged to pay for them.
- High unemployment also means less PAYE is collected as fewer people are working. Also, less VAT will be collected as the unemployed have less money to spend.

> **Exam Tip:** Outside of the short questions, any questions on this section have been general ones requiring some knowledge on various economic variables. However, a question can also be asked on specific variables such as inflation, interest rates or taxation. (See Question 2, 2006 exam.)

IMPACT OF BUSINESS ON THE DEVELOPMENT OF THE ECONOMY

Local impact

- **Employment** is created in the local area. This leads to a reduction in the numbers of unemployed and a reduction in social welfare payments.
- Business needs to be supplied with services by other firms, which leads to the establishment of **spin-off business**.

- As business grows in an area, the need for improved **infrastructure** increases. Thus, development of local transport, communications and other services improves with the business.
- An **entrepreneurial culture** is created when business develops in an area. This provides an incentive for others to follow.

National impact

- Business development creates **employment** on a national scale.
- An increase in business increases **tax revenue** collected by government. Employees pay more PAYE, more VAT is collected from purchases and companies pay corporation tax on their profits.
- Most of the multinationals that set up in Ireland export a large percentage of their output. This leads to an improvement in Ireland's **balance of trade** and **balance of payments**. Indigenous Irish firms also export some of their output.
- Ireland gets a **positive image** abroad as firms set up here. This helps to further attract more business to the country.

Some negative effects

- When multinationals set up in Ireland, they create intense **competition** with indigenous Irish firms. This may cause smaller Irish firms to close. For example, the arrival of Aldi and Lidl has led to the closure of some smaller grocery stores.
- An increase in business activity may have a negative impact on the **environment.** Some firms may dump illegally and cause pollution unless they are closely monitored.
- Some firms become very big and powerful and try to maximise profits at the expense of the consumer. For example, in the past, Vodafone and Bank of Ireland have been guilty of overcharging their customers.

EXAM QUESTIONS

Exam question 1

Analyse how the economic variables in the Irish economy have an impact on business activity. (25 marks)

Marking scheme
Four variables required at 7 marks, 6 marks, 6 marks and 6 marks. The split is **2 marks** for naming the variable and **5 marks/4 marks** for a development of it.

Sample answer

- **Inflation (2 marks):** This is an increase in the cost of living from one year to the next. If inflation is low, this has positive effects on business. Consumers will buy more goods and services, which will increase business profits. Low inflation also means that goods are cheaper to produce and as a result firms that are exporting are more competitive. **(5 marks)**
- **Interest rates (2 marks):** Ireland's interest rates are set by the ECB. If interest rates are low, consumers can borrow more cheaply, which means they will spend more. This is good for business. Low rates also mean that firms can borrow more cheaply, which allows them to expand the business and compete with international firms. **(4 marks)**
- **Exchange rates (2 marks):** Exchange rates affect firms that are involved in international trade with countries outside of the Eurozone. A firm exporting to the UK, for example, will favour a strong sterling in relation to the euro, whereas a firm importing raw materials from the UK will favour a weak sterling exchange rate. Changes in rates can affect company profits. **(4 marks)**
- **Taxation (2 marks):** Both business and individuals favour lower tax rates. If corporation tax is kept low, then company profits will be higher, which helps the long-term security of business. If PAYE rates are low, then workers have more disposable income. As a result, they will spend more, which adds to business profits. **(4 marks)**

6.5: GOVERNMENT AND BUSINESS

REASONS FOR GOVERNMENT INVOLVEMENT IN BUSINESS

- To develop the state's **natural resources**. Resources such as the natural gas off Kinsale belong to all the citizens and the government develops this for the benefit of the country.
- The state became involved in business activity at a time when private enterprise could not have **afforded** to provide some services, e.g. air and rail transport, electricity generation.
- To provide **important services** to areas where they might not be profitable, e.g. electricity and transport to remote areas.
- To develop the **infrastructure** of the country, e.g. National Roads Authority.
- To **encourage** business development. Agencies such as the IDA and Enterprise Ireland help promote business activity in the country.
- In order to protect the **environment**, the government created the Environmental Protection Agency. This ensures that businesses are fulfilling their environmental responsibilities.

THE GOVERNMENT'S ROLE IN CREATING A SUITABLE CLIMATE FOR BUSINESS

Revenue and expenditure policies

Government spending has the following effects on business:

- **Sales and profits:** The government is the largest buyer of goods and services in the country. This is very profitable for firms that supply these goods and services.
- **Capital spending:** Government spending on capital projects such as new hospitals, schools, roads, etc. is a major contributor to the success of the construction and engineering industries. Both direct and indirect employment is created.
- **Grants:** The government provides a wide range of grants and incentives to encourage business to set up. IDA Ireland attracts foreign firms to Ireland, while Enterprise Ireland provides assistance to indigenous industries.

Taxation policies

- **Corporation tax:** As of 2006, the rate of corporation tax is 12.5 per cent. This low rate allows businesses to retain a large proportion of their profits for reinvestment and expansion. It is also responsible for many foreign firms setting up in Ireland.
- **PAYE:** By keeping income tax rates low (20 per cent and 42 per cent as of 2006), the government increases workers' disposable incomes. This benefits the business community, as more money will be spent on goods and services. Lower income tax rates also create a stable industrial relations climate.
- **VAT:** Low rates of VAT benefit businesses, as consumers have greater spending power.

Government economic planning

Government economic planning reduces uncertainty for business. Every three years, the **social partners** get together to negotiate National Agreements. The social partners are the government, trade unions, employers' groups, e.g. IBEC, social and community groups and the Irish Farmers Association. Issues negotiated are wages, taxes and social welfare payments.

These agreements help business in the following ways.

- Industries can plan production costs more accurately if wage costs are known.
- Industrial relations stability is ensured as all parties agree pay increases.

Infrastructural development

In order to create a suitable climate for business, a well-developed infrastructure is essential. The government's role is to ensure that efficient transport, communications, energy and financial services industries exist to support business. Major developments have taken place, e.g. Dublin Port Tunnel, a new terminal for Dublin Airport, broadband in all towns, etc.

Government departments and agencies

- **IDA Ireland:** Encourages foreign firms to set up in Ireland. It offers grants and financial incentives to firms that set up here. This helps to create jobs.
- **Enterprise Ireland:** Provides a number of supports for indigenous industries such as grants, advice, help with business plans, training, marketing assistance, etc.
- **Labour Court and Labour Relations Commission:** These two bodies provide an important service for business in the state by resolving industrial relations problems at an early stage. They help create a stable industrial relations climate.
- **FÁS:** The national training agency. Firms looking for workers with certain skills can contact FÁS.
- **County Enterprise Boards (CEBs):** The CEBs help encourage business at a local level. They provide grants, advice, training and mentoring services to small firms starting off and help them to get up and running.

GOVERNMENT'S ROLE IN REGULATING BUSINESS

Consumers

Business is regulated in how it deals with consumers through two main laws: the **Consumer Information Act** and the **Sale of Goods and Supply of Services Act.**

In addition to these, any firms involved in mergers or takeovers must get approval from the **Competition Authority** before agreement is reached. This is to ensure that the new business enterprise does not work against consumer interests.

Employees

Employees' rights are protected through the labour laws: the **Industrial Relations Act 1990, Unfair Dismissals Act 1977 and 1993** and **Employment Equality Act 1998.**

In addition to these laws, the **Health and Safety Authority** carries out inspections of workplaces to ensure that there are safe and healthy working conditions for employees.

Environment

There are strict regulations in place for businesses in relation to dumping, waste disposal, recycling, etc. These are enforced by the **Environmental Protection Agency (EPA)**.

The EPA is the government watchdog that ensures firms are complying with environmental laws. It can impose large fines on offending firms.

General public

The rights of the general public are also protected by government regulation. For example, the **Data Protection Act 1988** set up the **Data Protection Agency**. It outlines the rights of all people on whom electronic data is held.

ROLE OF THE GOVERNMENT AS AN EMPLOYER

The government is the largest single employer by far. Some 350,000 people work in government jobs in some capacity. Government employment falls into the following categories:

- **Public sector workforce**, such as civil servants, teachers, gardaí and nurses. This includes all those working in local authorities, county councils and corporations.
- **Employment in state-sponsored bodies** such as the ESB, An Post and Dublin Bus.
- There are also thousands of **jobs created indirectly** in areas such as catering, cleaning and providing other services to the government.

PRIVATISATION

Privatisation is the sale of a state-owned company by the government to private investors. The company gets a quotation on the stock exchange and becomes a public limited company (PLC). The two most recent privatisations were Telecom Éireann (which became Eircom) in 1999 and Aer Lingus in 2006.

Reasons for and benefits of privatisation

- It is argued that running companies is not the business of government. Therefore, they should be privatised and run professionally by business managers.
- Since they are not completely profit driven, state-owned firms are not as efficient as they could be. Some of them make losses. The **taxpayers** pay for these losses.
- Privatisation raises a huge amount of **capital** for the government, which can be used to repay debt, reduce taxes or pay for government spending in other areas.
- Due to **global competition**, it is necessary for firms to become extremely **efficient**. Privatisation will achieve this, as shareholders who have profit as the main objective now own the company.
- As a result of being privatised, these companies will now have greater access to **finance for expansion**. They can issue more shares to raise finance or get loan capital from banks.
- Being a PLC on the stock exchange means that the company will now be able to attract **top management** to the firm. This can help to ensure its success.

Drawbacks of privatisation

- Privatised firms will try to make as much profit as possible for the shareholders. This may result in a **loss of some services** in unprofitable areas.
- In order to maximise profits, privatised firms will cut costs. Part of this cost cutting may include making staff **redundant**.
- Once privatised, these firms may become targets for **takeovers** by international firms. For example, Eircom PLC was taken over by the Australian bank Babcock and Brown.
- **Prices** may rise as a result of privatisation due to a policy of profit maximisation to keep the shareholders happy.

EXAM QUESTIONS

Exam question 1

Analyse how the Irish government creates a suitable climate for business in the state. Use examples in the analysis. (25 marks)

Marking scheme

Four points at 7 marks, 6 marks, 6 marks and 6 marks. The marks are split into **3 marks** for introducing the point, **3 marks/2 marks** for a brief development of the point and **1 mark** for an example. The example may well be included in the development.

Sample answer

- The government spends billions of euro every year, through capital and current spending, on goods and services. (**3 marks**) This is a great boost to all the firms that supply these goods and services. Capital spending on roads, schools, hospitals, etc. contributes to the success of the construction, engineering and tourism industries. (**3 marks**) For example, improvements in airports mean more tourists. (**1 mark**)
- A good climate for business can be created by government fiscal (taxation) policy. (**3 marks**) If PAYE rates are low, then workers have greater take-home pay and a better industrial relations climate exists. Also, they will spend more on goods and services. (**2 marks**) Rates are presently 20 per cent and 42 per cent. (**1 mark**)
- By keeping the corporation tax rate low, the government encourages the development of business. (**3 marks**) A low corporation tax also attracts foreign firms into Ireland, which provide a lot of employment and spin-off business. (**2 marks**) The rate is currently 12.5 per cent. (**1 mark**)
- The climate for business is helped by major improvements to the infrastructure. (**3 marks**) Major spending takes place on roads, communications, etc., which helps business to function more efficiently. (**2 marks**) For example, Dublin Port Tunnel has eased congestion in Dublin. (**1 mark**)

6.6: SOCIAL RESPONSIBILITIES OF BUSINESS

Business ethics

Ethics are moral principles that are concerned with right and wrong and honesty and fairness. Business ethics refer to how people both inside and outside the business are treated by the business. Just because a practice is legal does not mean that it is ethical. Businesses should have a **code of ethics**. This is a written statement outlining the behaviour expected of the business in its dealings with stakeholders. It is like a rulebook of right and wrong.

Encouraging ethical behaviour

- If the managing director provides **ethical leadership**, this will rub off on the employees.
- The firm should have a **code of ethics** in the workplace.
- The staff is given information and **training** in ethical business practices.
- The firm should promote a policy of encouraging ethical practice among the staff and have a **reward** system in place for staff who behave ethically.
- Promote a **whistle-blowing** approach whereby staff members are encouraged to report any employees who are not behaving ethically.

Social responsibilities of business

The firm has social responsibilities to the following.
- **Customers:** The firm should provide a quality good or service at a reasonable price. All necessary information should be provided. The firm should also provide a proper after-sales service.
- **Employees:** Employees should have safe and healthy working conditions. They should be paid a fair wage. All employment legislation should be followed in the workplace.
- **Shareholders:** The board of directors should be open and honest with shareholders and keep them informed about developments affecting the company.
- **Suppliers:** Suppliers should be paid on time for goods supplied and treated fairly by the company.
- **Local community:** The local community and environment should be respected. Firms should give something back to the local communities in which they operate, e.g. sponsorship.
- **Government:** The firm should obey all government legislation. All taxes should be collected and corporation tax on profits should be paid on time.

Costs of being socially responsible

- Providing an after-sales service to **customers** costs the firm money, as does dealing with all complaints and providing redress for faulty goods or services.
- The firm must pay a fair wage (at least the minimum wage) and ensure there are safe and healthy working conditions. The social needs of the **employees** must also be met with social clubs, nights out, etc.
- A fair price should be paid to **suppliers** for materials. They should be paid on time, which may add to a firm's costs.
- Although not obliged to do so, companies often put something back into local **communities**, e.g. sponsorship of a local team.
- In order to protect the **environment**, the firm should try to recycle as much as possible. Safe dumping of all waste is also necessary, which adds to the firm's costs.

ENVIRONMENTAL ISSUES AND BUSINESS

- **Pollution:** Firms must be careful not to pollute the environment, e.g. air, water or noise pollution. Any firms found to be causing pollution will be fined by the Environmental Protection Agency (EPA).
- **Energy consumption:** Firms should be trying to conserve energy where possible. Oil, which is our main source of energy, will eventually run out. This means switching to renewable sources of energy such as wind and solar power.
- **Sustainable development:** Business, and society in general, should be aware that there is a responsibility to future generations to leave the earth in good condition. This involves using renewable sources of energy.
- **Climate change:** Global warming is the major environmental issue of the twenty-first century. Industry and business are contributing to this by damaging the ozone layer as a result of chemical emissions.
- **Dumping and waste disposal:** Vast amounts of waste are produced each year. Some firms dump some of this illegally in order to reduce costs.
- **Recycling:** Firms should recycle as much waste and packaging as possible. This reduces the need for dumping.

Characteristics of an environmentally conscious company

- **Openness and honesty:** Being open to new methods and new thinking on environmental issues and being honest with the stakeholders.
- **Awareness:** The firm is aware of the importance of the environment and promotes environmental awareness among its employees through talks and reminders posted in the workplace.
- **Consultation:** The local community and other stakeholders should be consulted on all environmental issues.

- **Environmental audit:** The firm will carry these out regularly to ensure they are operating in an environmentally friendly manner.
- **Recycling:** The firm will use materials and packaging that are recyclable and environmentally friendly. Correct waste disposal methods will be used.
- **Machinery and production:** Investment will take place in new, cleaner machinery, which reduces pollution. The use of chemical products will be minimised.

Costs for a business of being environmentally responsible

- **Cost increases:** New machinery and equipment have to be purchased to make production processes safe, e.g. reducing gas emissions. This will increase their costs.
- **EPA regulations:** The EPA issues pollution control licences to firms and can impose fines on firms that cause pollution. If taken to court, these firms may also incur legal expenses.
- **Adverse publicity:** The costs of getting a poor public image are difficult to measure, but may be great. If a firm gets a bad name in relation to environmental issues, their sales and profits will suffer.
- **Dumping and waste disposal:** This is a big cost to business. IBEC says that waste disposal is now the third biggest business expense after wages and insurance.
- **Green taxes:** If firms damage the environment in any way, the government may impose 'green' taxes on them. These taxes are part of the 'polluter pays' principle whereby firms may be fined and made to pay the costs of any clean-up of the environment.

Opportunities for firms in being environmentally responsible

- **Cost reductions:** The use of clean and more efficient production systems means that firms can often reduce their costs as they move from older, dirtier and less efficient methods.
- **New business opportunities:** New technologies and methods used to reduce and treat waste may become business opportunities in themselves. Examples include recycling firms.
- **Green consumers:** If firms have a good public image due to being environmentally conscious, then they will attract new customers.
- **Financial institutions:** These are sensitive to environmental issues and may have them as conditions to granting finance.
- **Employees:** A positive attitude to environmental issues is good for employee morale. Staff are happier working in clean, safe working conditions for a firm that cares about the environment.

Exam questions

Exam question 1

Describe the opportunities and costs for a business of meeting its environmental responsibilities.
(25 marks)

Marking scheme
Three opportunities and two costs or three costs and two opportunities at **5 marks** each. The 5 marks are split into **2 marks** and **3 marks.**

Sample answer
(The solution here lists three costs and two opportunities.)

- **Proper dumping and waste disposal (2 marks):** This is now one of the biggest costs for any firm. Much waste material now has to be recycled, which adds to the costs. Firms found to be dumping illegally will be fined by the EPA. **(3 marks)**
- **New machinery and equipment (2 marks):** Environmentally responsible firms will have clean and efficient equipment in order to make production processes safer, e.g. reducing gas emissions. This adds to the firm's costs. **(3 marks)**
- **Green taxes (2 marks):** If firms damage the environment, the government may impose 'green taxes' on them. This is a means of fining the firm, which may then also have to pay for the clean-up of any environmental damage. **(3 marks)**
- **Green consumers (2 marks):** Businesses that behave responsibly towards the environment will attract a large number of environmentally aware consumers. For any firms trading internationally, this green image is vital. **(3 marks)**
- **Cost reductions (2 marks):** Most firms that upgrade and change to cleaner, more environmentally friendly machinery find that it is more efficient and brings about cost reductions. **(3 marks)**

IMPORTANT DEFINITIONS FROM UNIT 6

- **Primary industries:** The extractive industries, e.g. agriculture, forestry, fishing and mining.
- **Secondary industries:** Manufacturing industries, e.g. indigenous firms, transnationals, agribusiness and the construction sector.
- **Services industry:** This is also known as the tertiary sector and includes sectors such as transport, communications, banking, IT, retailing and leisure.
- **Indigenous firm:** Firms that are set up, owned and run by Irish people. They are home-grown Irish industries.
- **Memorandum of association:** This document outlines the relationship between the company and the public. It lists the amount of authorised share capital and a statement that the liability of the shareholders is limited.
- **Articles of association:** This contains the internal rules and regulations of the company. It outlines details of share capital, rules for calling meetings and procedures for electing directors.
- **Certificate of incorporation:** The 'birth certificate' of the company sent to it by the Companies Registration Office. The company now has a separate legal identity from its owners and can sue and be sued in its own name.
- **Limited liability:** Shareholders only lose the amount of their investment if a company fails. Their own private assets cannot be called upon to pay off company debts.
- **Alliance:** A partnership agreement between two firms for the mutual benefit of both. Both firms remain separate entities.
- **Franchise:** This is when an established business allows another person to set up and use its name in exchange for a fee and an annual percentage of the sales. An exact formula is followed.
- **Transnational:** A firm with its headquarters in one country and branches in many other countries. It is also called a multinational.
- **Privatisation:** The sale of a state firm by the government to private investors. The new company becomes a public limited company (PLC) on the stock exchange.
- **Community development:** This involves local people developing the local area in the way that best suits the community. Groups of people help themselves and their communities by setting up enterprises, schemes and projects.
- **Inflation:** An increase in the cost of living from one year to the next. Prices in general are rising, but not all prices rise. The Consumer Price Index (CPI) measures inflation.
- **Exchange rates:** The rates at which one currency can be exchanged for another. They are the value of currencies in relation to other currencies.
- **Privatisation:** The sale of a state-owned company by the government to private investors. The company becomes a public limited company (PLC) on the stock exchange.
- **Business ethics:** Moral principles by which a business decides what is right and wrong. Just because something is legal for a business does not mean that it is ethical.
- **Code of ethics:** A written statement outlining the behaviour expected of the business in its dealings with stakeholders. It is like a rulebook of right and wrong.
- **Sustainable development:** This means operating a business in a manner that protects the environment for future generations. It involves using renewable sources of energy.

CHAPTER 7

Unit 7: The International Trading Environment

7.1: THE INTERNATIONAL TRADING ENVIRONMENT

THE SIGNIFICANCE OF INTERNATIONAL TRADE FOR THE IRISH ECONOMY

- **Open economy:** Because Ireland is such a small country and an island nation, it has an open economy. It depends on imports and exports to a much greater degree than most other countries.
- **Balance of trade and balance of payments:** When Irish firms export goods and services abroad, our BOT and BOP are improved (see overleaf).
- **Deregulation:** This is the elimination of barriers to trade. This is one of the main ideals of the EU. It means that Irish firms can import and export freely. The World Trade Organization (WTO) promotes deregulation.
- **Economies of scale:** The Irish market alone is too small for firms to achieve economies of scale. In order to achieve these cost savings, firms must be producing in large quantities, which means producing for international markets.
- **Choice and variety:** Countries and consumers enjoy a wide variety of goods that are available from other countries but cannot be produced domestically because of climate or lack of factors of production.
- **Competition:** Both new and established Irish firms are now exposed to competition from foreign firms. There is no government protection. As a result, some Irish firms will go out of business, causing job losses.

Exam Tip: Five points should be sufficient.

- **Visible trade:** This is the import and export of **goods.**
- **Invisible trade:** This is the import and export or **services.**

TABLE 7.1: BALANCE OF TRADE AND BALANCE OF PAYMENTS

	EXPORTS	**IMPORTS**
Visible	• Export of goods. • Money comes into Ireland. • Example: Sale of farm machinery to Spain.	• Import of goods. • Money leaves Ireland. • Example: Purchase of wine from Italy.
Invisible	• Export of services. • Money comes into Ireland. • Example: Foreign travellers using Ryanair.	• Import of services. • Money leaves Ireland. • Example: Irish people going on holidays abroad.

- **Balance of trade** = visible exports – visible imports
- **Balance of payments** = all exports (visible + invisible) – all imports (visible + invisible)

Sample question

From the following information, calculate the balance of trade and the balance of payments: visible exports €200 million, invisible exports €45 million, invisible imports €30 million, visible imports €180 million.

- Balance of trade = €200m – €180m = €20m surplus.
- Balance of payments = (€200m + €45m) – (€180m + €30m) = €35m surplus.

THE CHANGING NATURE OF THE INTERNATIONAL ECONOMY AND ITS EFFECTS ON IRISH BUSINESS

- **Globalisation:** The treatment of the world as a single market by large companies. These companies produce and sell the same standardised products all over the world, e.g. Pepsi, McDonald's, Nike.
- **Increased use of technology:** Communications have improved greatly due to improvements in IT. Firms are in instant contact with their markets. Most firms have websites and advertise and sell over the internet. This is called e-commerce.
- **Increased levels of competition:** As a result of free trade, there is pressure on Irish firms to be efficient in order to compete with foreign firms. Less efficient firms will close down.
- **Deregulation:** This means the opening up of international trade by removing barriers to trade. Irish firms have to become very efficient to survive.

- **Trading blocs:** A trading bloc is a group of countries that organise free trade among the members. Ireland is a member of the EU and can sell to other EU members without restriction.
- **Emerging economies:** Economies such as India and China are developing rapidly. These countries offer huge opportunities for Irish companies to develop markets into.
- **Enlarging European Union:** There is a huge population in Eastern Europe, which offers great opportunities for Irish firms to export into. There is a shortage of many goods and services in these countries.
- **Inward migration:** As a result of EU accession, tens of thousands of Eastern Europeans are working in Ireland due to the attractive wage levels. In future, though, this may put pressure on Irish jobs.

Exam Tip: Five points would probably be sufficient.

OPPORTUNITIES AND CHALLENGES FOR IRISH BUSINESS IN INTERNATIONAL TRADE

Opportunities for Irish business

- **Larger markets:** The Irish market has just over 4 million people and Irish firms cannot depend on it alone. The EU has a large and growing market as new Eastern European countries join up.
- **Deregulation:** Irish firms can trade with other EU members without restrictions. These include the new Eastern European members, which have a huge demand for goods and services.
- **Expansion:** Irish firms have an opportunity to expand their businesses abroad. As this happens they may achieve economies of scale, which reduces unit costs and improves efficiency.
- **English language:** English is the international business language, which gives Irish firms a head start in international trade.
- **Technology:** Developments in ICT have reduced Ireland's disadvantage of being on the periphery of Europe. For firms that sell services, location is now unimportant. Most firms now do business over the internet.
- **Green image:** Ireland retains a 'green' image abroad. This helps to promote our tourism and food manufacturing industries.

Challenges facing Irish business in international trade

- **Competition:** Irish firms are expected to compete with foreign industries on an equal footing. As a result of foreign competition, only the most efficient firms will survive.

- **High cost base:** The costs of running a business in Ireland are high. Wages and insurance costs are among the highest in Europe. This makes it difficult for exporters to compete with goods from low-wage countries.
- **Distribution costs:** Being an island on the edge of Europe means that costs of transportation for exporters are higher than for many of their competitors.
- **Payment difficulties:** Firms that trade internationally may have difficulties getting paid by foreign firms. Some may suffer bad debts, which can badly affect profits.
- **Language difficulties:** With so many different languages in the EU alone, Irish exporters face problems with product names, marketing, selling, etc.
- **Knowledge of foreign markets:** Most Irish firms will not be familiar with foreign markets and differences in customs and cultures, tastes, geography, etc.

Trading blocs

A trading bloc is a group of countries that agree to trade together without any barriers. The aim is to have free movement of goods, services, labour and capital. They agree to have common trade barriers with non-members of the bloc. The EU and the World Trade Organization (WTO) are examples of trading blocs.

WORLD TRADE ORGANIZATION

The WTO was set up in 1995 to promote free trade among its members. Its main aims are to:
- Promote free trade worldwide by eliminating barriers to trade.
- Remove subsidies to the agricultural sector.
- Remove any special trading agreements between countries.
- Protect intellectual property rights worldwide, e.g. copyrights.

EXAM QUESTIONS

Exam question 1

Evaluate the opportunities and challenges for Irish businesses that engage in international trade. Refer to the enlargement of the European Union in your answer. (30 marks)

Marking scheme
Five points at **6 marks** each: three opportunities and two challenges or three challenges and two opportunities. The 6 marks are split into **3 marks** for an introduction of the point and **3 marks** for a development of it.

Sample answer

- Irish exporters have access to larger markets. (**3 marks**) The Irish market is very small compared to the huge EU market. By selling to existing and new EU member states, Irish firms diversify the risk attached to selling to just one market. (**3 marks**)
- Irish firms can expand and achieve economies of scale. (**3 marks**) The emerging economies of Eastern Europe offer opportunities for Irish firms to expand into. Large populations in these countries have a desire for Western goods and services. This will allow Irish firms to produce on a larger scale and achieve economies of scale. (**3 marks**)
- Deregulation and free trade. (**3 marks**) When the new countries join the EU trading bloc, all barriers to trade are removed. This means free movement of goods, services and labour between Ireland and these states, which makes international trade easy. (**3 marks**)
- There is increased competition for Irish firms as a result of the enlarging EU. (**3 marks**) All EU member states can now export freely into Ireland. This poses a threat to Irish firms, which have to become more efficient to survive. (**3 marks**)
- There are different customs and cultures in different member states, especially the newer members. (**3 marks**) In order to trade successfully with these countries, Irish firms have to gain knowledge of these customs and cultures and how they do business. (**3 marks**)

7.2: THE EUROPEAN UNION

THE IMPORTANCE OF THE EUROPEAN UNION

The EU is an economic and political union. Its aim is to have free trade in goods, services, labour and capital. One of the main objectives of the EU is to create a single market throughout the member states.

SINGLE EUROPEAN MARKET (SEM)

The SEM came into effect on 1 January 1993 as a result of the Single European Act.

Opportunities for Irish business as a result of the SEM

- **Huge market:** The huge EU market is now open for Irish business to export into. This market has grown with the new accession states. As a result, dependence on the home market is reduced.

- **Economies of scale:** When firms start to produce for the huge EU market, they can achieve economies of scale. This helps to make Irish firms more competitive.
- **Expansion:** As Irish firms export more goods to the European market, they can expand. As they get bigger, they become more competitive with international firms.
- **Public procurement:** All EU firms can tender for foreign government contracts in any EU countries. Governments cannot favour firms in their own country. This means Irish firms may get government contracts in other EU countries.
- **Inward investment:** As a result of EU membership, many transnationals from outside the EU have located in Ireland. This has created many jobs.
- **Funding:** Huge amounts of structural funding have been made available to Ireland from the EU, which has led to major infrastructural improvements.
- **Deregulation:** The removal of barriers to trade has led to a reduction in the costs of exporting for Irish firms. This has been brought about by less documentation and simplified customs procedures.

Challenges facing Irish business as a result of the SEM

- **Competition:** Foreign imports are now competing directly with Irish goods, which means competition for Irish firms. Less efficient firms will close down.
- **Exporting costs:** The costs of exporting from Ireland are quite high when transport costs are included. This adds to the cost of selling goods abroad.
- **Public procurement:** Foreign firms can now tender for Irish government contracts. Irish firms are no longer guaranteed to get the job.
- **Capital:** In order to remain competitive, many firms have had to expand and achieve economies of scale. This involves getting large amounts of capital.
- **Staffing:** As a result of the SEM, Irish people can work abroad as easily as at home. This may lead to a shortage of qualified people in Ireland.

Exam Tip: Most questions on this section look for a **combination** of both opportunities and challenges. If this was the case, six points in total would be enough (three opportunities and three challenges).

THE INSTITUTIONS OF THE EUROPEAN UNION

European Commission

This is the management body of the EU and comprises commissioners who are selected by the governments of each state. As of 2006, the Irish Commissioner is Charlie McCreevy.

Role of the Commission

- **Proposals:** The Commission draws up proposals for new EU laws, which are then debated by the Parliament.
- **Enforcement:** Implements EU policies and enforces existing EU law. Has the power to impose fines on companies breaking EU law.
- **Guardian of the treaties:** Ensures that all member states are implementing the rules and regulations laid down by the EU. If any member states breach agreements, the Commission can fine them or refer the matter to the Court of Justice.
- **Defence of EU interests:** Acts in the best interests of the EU. Acts as a mediator to resolve disputes between member states.
- **EU budget:** Draws up and manages the budget of the EU.

European Parliament

The EU Parliament is elected directly by the voters and as a result represents the citizens of the EU. The elected members are called MEPs (Member of European Parliament).

Role of the Parliament

- **Represents:** Directly represents the citizens of the EU, as the MEPs are elected by the citizens of each member country.
- **Legislative:** Parliament debates new legislation put forward by the Commission. It gives its opinion on these new proposals and can put forward amendments to any new laws.
- **Supervisory function:** Parliament supervises the work of the Commission and vets and appoints members of the Commission. It even has the power to dismiss the Commission.
- **Budgetary function:** Parliament approves and has the power to amend the EU budget. It monitors all budgetary spending by the EU.

Council of Ministers

This is the main decision-making body of the EU. It comprises the minister from each country for the area under discussion, e.g. if a health issue is under discussion, then the health ministers from all member states will be present.

Role of the Council

- The Council is the supreme law-making body of the EU.
- Policies that have been proposed by the Commission and debated by Parliament are sent to the Council of Ministers to be decided on.
- Sets down the economic and political objectives for the EU.
- Makes all the key economic and political decisions of the EU.
- Works toward co-operation between member states on European issues.

Court of Justice

The function of the Court of Justice is to ensure that EU law is observed in all member states.

Role of the Court
- Interprets and explains EU law for member states, companies and individual citizens.
- Adjudicates on disputes between the other institutions of the EU, e.g. Commission and Council.
- Ensures that EU law is observed in all member states and adjudicates on cases that come before it.
- Determines the legality of acts of the Commission.

Court of Auditors

The Court of Auditors is responsible for managing the Community finances. This is important in order to prevent fraud.

Role of the Court of Auditors
- Ensures that the budget was spent as it should have been.
- Carries out spot checks at various levels throughout the EU to ensure that no fraud is taking place.
- Prepares an annual report for the Parliament and Council showing its findings.

POLICIES OF THE EUROPEAN UNION AND THEIR EFFECT ON IRISH BUSINESS

Common Agricultural Policy (CAP)

The CAP is based on three principles:
- **Single market:** All agricultural produce is to move freely within the EU with common prices and common rules of competition.
- **Financial solidarity:** The EU will continue to finance the CAP for the foreseeable future. However, the guaranteed price supports to farmers have been abolished.
- **EU preference:** Preference is given to the sale of EU products within the EU. Tariffs are placed on all non-EU produce entering the bloc.

In 2005, the CAP was radically changed. The previous system of providing subsidies to farmers to guarantee them a minimum price was abolished. It was replaced with a single annual payment to farmers, regardless of production. Thus, the link between production and payment was broken. This is called decoupling. From 2005, farmers produce 'for the market', i.e. they produce only what they think they can sell. This means that the more efficient farmers will prosper while the small, inefficient farmers will be forced to leave farming.

Competition Policy

The following areas are covered:

- **Cartels:** A cartel exists when firms collude together to fix prices or share markets. This is forbidden under the Competition Policy.
- **Dominant position:** If a firm has a dominant position in the market, it cannot abuse this position by restricting competition. It is not an offence to have a dominant position, but it is illegal to exploit or abuse it.
- **Mergers and takeovers:** All mergers and takeovers must be referred to the Commission for investigation before being allowed to go ahead. If a dominant position will result, then the deal may not be allowed.
- **Government aid:** National governments are forbidden from providing financial assistance to state-owned or other companies if the effect is to give them an advantage over rival companies.
- **Public procurement:** All government contracts must be open to all companies from all member states. No national government can show preference to a company from its own country when offering contracts for work.
- **Deregulation:** All firms holding monopolies, whether state owned or private, must deregulate, i.e. allow other firms to enter the market.

Common Fisheries Policy

The main provisions are:

- **Access to fishing grounds:** Each state has a 19 km fishing zone around the coast into which foreign boats are forbidden from entering.
- **Total allowable catch:** There are quotas on the quantities of certain species that can be caught. This prevents overfishing and helps to preserve stocks.
- **Structural policies:** Grants are available from the EU for the construction of new vessels. Funding is also available for port development.
- **Monitoring fishing activity:** The EU provides funding for the purchase of fishery protection vessels and aircraft. The skippers must record all fish catches.
- **Marketing of fisheries products:** This is designed to stabilise the market, ensure a steady supply of products and reasonable prices for consumers.

Social Policy (Social Charter)

Basic principles of the Social Policy include:
- The right to work in the EU country of one's choice.
- The right to a fair wage and good working conditions and safety at work.
- The right of men and women to equal treatment.
- Positive discrimination for employment of the disabled.
- The rights of workers to information, consultation and participation in the workplace.
- The protection of children and adolescents.
- The guarantee of minimum living standards for the elderly.
- The rights of the unemployed to training and opportunities to return to the workforce.

Economic and Monetary Union

The European Central Bank (ECB) was established to operate a single monetary policy for the EU. The aims are:
- A common EU currency called the euro.
- Creating a single monetary policy for the EU. The ECB implements this policy. The aim is to have price stability in the EU.
- Creating common economic and budgetary policies. This includes having stable inflation rates.

Benefits of the EMU to Ireland
- **Common currency:** Importing and exporting is a lot easier. Irish firms no longer have to incur the costs of changing money, nor are they exposed to exchange rate fluctuations.
- **Low inflation:** The ECB seeks to keep inflation rates in the Eurozone low and stable. This should lead to firms in member states being competitive with firms outside the zone.
- **Interest rates:** Interest rates are similar in member states. This leads to freer movement of capital within the zone.
- **Price comparisons:** The euro makes price comparisons easy within the zone. This allows consumers to find the best value.
- **Foreign direct investment:** Due to the common currency, many transnationals are attracted to locate in Ireland. This creates jobs and wealth.

Possible drawbacks
- **The UK:** Ireland's biggest trading partner is outside the Eurozone. This means that a lot of the benefits of a common currency do not apply to much of Ireland's trade.

- **Loss of control:** Ireland no longer has any control over its interest rates since they are set by the ECB.
- **Competition:** The common currency means that many more imports are coming into Ireland. This puts pressure on indigenous Irish firms, which will have to be efficient to survive.

THE DECISION-MAKING PROCESS IN THE EUROPEAN UNION

PROPOSAL → CONSULTATION → REDRAFTING → APPROVAL → IMPLEMENTATION

- **Proposal:** The Commission has the right of initiative and proposes new legislation.
- **Consultation:** These proposals are sent to the Parliament for discussion and consultation. Some amendments are made at this stage. The proposal is returned to the Commission.
- **Redrafting:** The Commission redrafts the proposal and sends it to the Council of Ministers.
- **Approval:** The Council of Ministers makes a decision on the proposal. It may accept or reject it.
- **Implementation:** The Commission now implements the new law. It decides how it is to be implemented. It can be implemented in one of three ways:
  - ➤ **Regulation:** This is a law that applies throughout the EU with immediate effect. It takes precedence over national laws.
  - ➤ **Directive:** This aims to harmonise EU laws. Each member state must amend its own laws to comply with the Directive within a certain timeframe. Each government can implement the Directive in its own way.
  - ➤ **Decision:** This is a judgment by the EU binding only on the country, company or organisation to which it is directed.

Role of special interest groups

Interest groups are pressure groups that are formed to ensure that the people they represent have a voice and are not disadvantaged by government or EU decisions. They lobby and speak on behalf of the section of society that they represent.

Examples of interest groups include:
- **Irish Farmers Association (IFA):** Represents the interests of farmers.
- **Consumers Association of Ireland (CAI):** Represents the interests of consumers.

Interest groups:
- Lobby and put pressure on government ministers and EU representatives.
- Seek meetings with the decision makers in the EU institutions.

EXAM QUESTIONS

Exam question 1

Explain the importance for Ireland of: (a) any one of the policies of the European Union and (b) any one of the institutions of the European Union. (20 marks)

Marking scheme

The scheme here is a straightforward **10 marks** for a policy and **10 marks** for an institution. Each 10 marks is split into **2 marks** for naming the policy/institution, **4 marks** for a piece of information on it and **4 marks** for a second piece of information on it. The second piece of information should contain a reference to Ireland.

Exam question 2

Explain the decision-making process of the European Union. Include the relevant institutions in your answer. (25 marks)

Marking scheme

Five points at **5 marks** each. Your answer must include the three main institutions – Parliament, Commission and Council of Ministers.

Sample answer

- Proposals are made and/or drafted by the EU Commission. This is called the right of initiative. **(5 marks)**
- These proposals then go to the EU Parliament for consultation and discussion. Some amendments may be made at this stage. **(5 marks)**
- The proposals are returned to the Commission for redrafting. After this, the Commission sends them to the Council of Ministers. **(5 marks)**
- The Council makes a decision on the proposal. It may accept or reject it. This is called the approval stage. **(5 marks)**
- The proposal has now become law and is implemented by the Commission. It may become a Regulation, a Directive or a Decision. **(5 marks)**

7.3: INTERNATIONAL BUSINESS

THE GLOBAL MARKETING OF PRODUCTS AND SERVICES

A global company is one that treats the whole world as one huge single marketplace. Examples of global businesses are Intel, Shell, Microsoft and Coca Cola.

Characteristics of global business

- **Global market:** Identifies the world as its market, not any individual country. The firm then mass produces goods and sells them all over the world.
- **Standardised goods:** Large amounts of identical goods are mass produced and sold. Customers know exactly what they are getting, e.g. McDonald's. Slightly different varieties are produced for some countries.
- **Branding:** Global firms spend huge amounts of money on getting brand recognition for their goods. Their advertising campaigns cost millions of euro, e.g. Pepsi, Coca Cola.
- **Economies of scale:** Global companies have low production costs per unit as they benefit from economies of scale.

Factors giving rise to global companies

- **Own market saturation:** Many companies that are expanding find that growth is hindered by the size of the domestic market. The only way to continue their expansion is to export.
- **Economies of scale:** Production technologies have improved greatly, which makes the cost per unit of production cheaper and encourages firms to expand internationally.
- **Information and communications technology (ICT):** Due to rapid improvements in ICT, firms find it easier to get information on foreign markets. As a result of this and the increasing use of the internet, more firms are trading internationally and going global.
- **Deregulation:** As a result of barriers to trade being broken down all over the world, a global trading environment is created. The WTO is responsible for removing barriers to trade.
- **Emerging markets:** Countries with huge populations, e.g. China and India, have emerged onto the world business stage. These markets provide the opportunity for large firms to expand even more and become global firms.

OPPORTUNITIES AND THREATS OF GLOBAL MARKETING FOR IRISH BUSINESS

Opportunities for Irish business

- **Larger markets:** Firms that go global are no longer dependent on the small Irish market to sell their goods into. This will lead to a big increase in sales and profits.
- **Economies of scale:** As a result of producing and selling on a large scale, Irish firms can achieve economies of scale.
- **Brand recognition:** By exporting goods and services, Irish firms increase their brand recognition. As brand recognition grows, many customers will develop loyalty to these brands, which will create repeat business.
- **Expansion:** Doing business globally allows Irish companies to expand and become competitive with international firms. This safeguards their survival in the marketplace.

Threats to Irish business

- **Competition:** Irish firms that grow and become global companies will have to compete with some of the biggest firms in the world. This means having to improve quality and become more efficient.
- **Promotion:** Global firms spend huge amounts of money on advertising and promotion. This poses a challenge to Irish firms that are trying to compete with these firms, as the Irish firms must also have large promotion budgets.
- **Size:** Irish firms are naturally smaller than most international firms, which may put them at a competitive disadvantage.
- **Standardisation:** Irish firms have to have standardised products in order to compete globally. This means they will now have to mass produce goods for the global market.

GLOBAL MARKETING MIX

This involves applying the four Ps (product, price, promotion, place) to international marketing.
- **Global product:** The global product is a standardised one that is mass produced. It is sold throughout the world with the same design and features. Sometimes the product has to be slightly adapted to take different cultures or customs into account.
- **Global price:** Prices charged may have to be changed in come countries due to a number of factors, e.g. standards of living may be different in different markets, there may be additional marketing costs involved, there may be tariffs in some countries or transport and distributions costs may add to the price.
- **Global promotion:** Global firms spend millions of euro each year promoting their products. The firm may have a standardised or adapted marketing strategy. The firm

has to take language translation, cultural differences and possible legislation in other countries relating to advertising into account.

- **Global place:** This involves the channels of distribution used. Firms involved in foreign trade often use agents in their foreign markets. Sometimes a firm sets up a foreign subsidiary to distribute the goods or a firm may enter into a joint venture/ alliance with a foreign company that will produce and/or sell the goods abroad.

THE ROLE OF INFORMATION TECHNOLOGY IN GLOBALISATION

- **Access of information:** Firms can access information from the world's different markets quickly and cheaply. This information can be used to make business decisions.
- **Linking suppliers and customers:** Global companies often buy raw materials from other countries for use in production. Using EDI systems, this process is made easier as orders are automatically sent.
- **Video conferencing:** Management meetings can take place using video link-ups between different branches. This cuts down on the need for expensive and time-consuming travel.
- **E-business:** Many global firms now do business online. They advertise and promote their goods on their website and customers can place orders and pay by credit card.
- **Design:** New products can be designed and redesigned using the most cutting-edge technology. As customers' needs and wants change, products are changed to suit.

THE DEVELOPMENT AND IMPACT OF TRANSNATIONAL COMPANIES

Transnationals/multinationals are companies with headquarters in one country and branches in many other countries. Examples in Ireland include Intel, Hewlett Packard and Google.

Impact of transnationals in Ireland

- Transnationals create a lot of **employment**. This improves standards of living and creates wealth in the country.
- Much of what transnationals produce is exported. This contributes to an improvement in the **balance of trade** and the **balance of payments**.
- Transnationals produce huge amounts of **tax revenue** for the government. This includes PAYE, VAT and corporation taxes.
- As a result of their location here, **spin-off business** is created, as Irish firms are needed to supply the transnationals with essential goods and services.
- They bring new **management skills** and experience into Ireland. Irish firms may be able to learn from management techniques.

- They provide intense **competition** for indigenous Irish firms. Some of the less efficient ones may be forced to close if they cannot compete.
- Most of these firms **repatriate** at least some of their **profits** to their home country. This means the benefits do not remain in Ireland and represents a drain from the Irish economy.
- Transnationals have **no sense of loyalty** to Ireland. They often move out of a country to go to lower-wage economies. This can cause widespread unemployment in an area.
- The **raw materials** used by the multinationals are often bought in from the home or other country.

EXAM QUESTIONS

Exam question 1

Explain the importance of global marketing in international business. Use relevant examples in your answer. (20 marks)

Marking scheme

Four points are needed at **5 marks** each. A definition of global marketing is acceptable for one of the 5 marks. The 5 marks are split into **3 marks** for making a point and **2 marks** for a development/example.

Sample answer

- Global marketing involves a company treating the whole world as its market. A standardised product is produced for the world market, e.g. Coca Cola. **(5 marks)**
- Global marketing allows firms to achieve cost efficiencies and economies of scale. **(3 marks)** Producing for a world market allows for long production runs of standardised products, which results in cost savings. **(2 marks)**
- Global standardisation means that businesses do not consider the differences between countries and cultures to be important. **(3 marks)** Products are produced and promoted under a common world brand name, e.g. McDonald's. **(2 marks)**
- Global firms adopt a global marketing mix. **(3 marks)** This involves a standardised product (sometimes adapted to suit regional differences), common price, worldwide promotion and distribution to all corners of the globe. **(2 marks)**

IMPORTANT DEFINITIONS FROM UNIT 7

- **Deregulation:** The removal of barriers to trade between countries. It results in the free movement of goods, capital and labour.
- **Balance of trade:** The difference between the value of Ireland's exports and imports of goods. The BOT measures visible trade. BOT = visible exports – visible imports.
- **Balance of payments:** The difference between the value of all of Ireland's exports and all of Ireland's imports. It measures visible plus invisible trade. BOP = all exports – all imports.
- **Trading bloc:** A group of countries that agree to trade together without any barriers to trade. An example of a trading bloc is the EU.
- **Single European Market (SEM):** The creation of a single free trade area between all twenty-five member states of the EU. These countries trade together without any barriers to trade.
- **Global marketing:** Selling one product in the same way worldwide and treating the world as one large marketplace. A standardised product is produced and marketed under a common brand name, e.g. Coca Cola.
- **Transnational:** A company with its headquarters in one country and branches in many other countries. They are also called multinationals, e.g. Shell Oil.

CHAPTER 8
Sample Applied Business Question

SECTION 2

(80 marks)

This is a compulsory question based on units 4, 5, and 6 for the 2007 exam.

Applied Business Question

IMAGE PAINTS LTD

Image Paints Ltd is an Irish-owned paints manufacturer based in a north Dublin suburb. Paddy Farrell and John Dillon, two friends who had their own painting and decorating business, founded it fourteen years ago. From small beginnings, the business has grown rapidly, and now employs seventy workers in a large factory in an industrial estate. Image sells mainly to paint and DIY shops but also has a large retail outlet that sells directly to painters. The firm is known all along the east coast and has four vans on the road.

As a result of the construction boom in Ireland, Image has been doing extremely well. Paddy and John are good businessmen and are also very ambitious. For some time now they have been considering expanding the business. Two years ago, in order to facilitate their expansion, they admitted two new shareholders as investors. They have looked at many options for expansion but are undecided as to how they might proceed. There are a number of smaller painting and decorating stores in the area and another large paint manufacturer on the south side of Dublin.

Image employs a human resource manager and as a result a good industrial relations climate exists in the company. Most workers live within a two-mile radius of the factory. The staff has a social committee that organises nights out. Regular customers have an account with the firm and get decent discounts on bulk purchases. Some years ago, locals complained about fish dying in a nearby stream. Local community groups met with management of the factory and were assured that the company was following good environmental practices.

(a) Outline the various types of taxes and types of insurance which you would expect Image to be familiar with. Support your answer with reference to the text. (20 marks)

(b) Discuss **two** methods of expansion that Image could use to successfully expand the business. Make any relevant assumptions that you feel may be necessary. (30 marks)

(c) Evaluate the effects on Image's costs of meeting its social and environmental responsibilities. (30 marks)

(80 marks)

> **Exam Tip:** Students should read the **questions** of the ABQ before reading the text. This means that when you read the text, you read it looking for something definite. This can be done with each of the three parts.

Marking scheme

(a) **Three** taxes and **two** insurances or **two** taxes and **three** insurances are needed at **4 marks** each. The 4 marks is split into **2 marks** for naming the tax/insurance and **2 marks** for making a valid connection to the text.

(b) **Two** methods of expansion at **15 marks** each. The 15 marks is split into **5 marks** for naming the method of expansion, **5 marks** for a piece of information on the method and **5 marks** for making a valid connection to the text.

(c) **Three** effects on costs and **two** effects on opportunities or vice versa at **6 marks** each. The 6 marks is split into **4 marks** for an effect on costs/opportunity and **2 marks** for making a tie to the text. (At least two points must be related to the environment.)

Sample answer

(a) • **Pay as you earn (PAYE) (2 marks):** Image employs seventy people and will have to deduct this tax from their wages and send it on to the Inland Revenue. (**2 marks**)

• **VAT (2 marks):** This is Value Added Tax and Image will have to pay it on purchases and will charge it on sales to customers. (**2 marks**)

• **Corporation tax (2 marks):** Since Image is a limited company, it will have to pay corporation tax on its profits. (**2 marks**)

• **Employer's liability (2 marks):** Image has seventy staff and will need insurance cover in case any of them have an accident on the premises and claims from the company. (**2 marks**)

• **Motor insurance (2 marks):** We are told in the passage that Image has 'four vans on the road'. Therefore, they must have at least third party insurance. (**2 marks**)

(b) (i) **Alliance (5 marks):** This is when two businesses join together for the mutual benefit of both. It is not a permanent arrangement and can be ended at any time. Both firms remain separate entities. (**5 marks**) Image could form an alliance with the 'large paint manufacturer on the south side of Dublin'. Both firms would benefit from the expertise of the other and both would retain their own identities. (**5 marks**)

(ii) **Takeover (5 marks):** This is when one business gets control of another by buying out the shareholding (at least 51 per cent) of the other business. Complete control passes to the buying firm. (**5 marks**) This could be a suitable option for Image, as there are a 'number of smaller painting and decorating stores in the area'. This would give Image a retail presence along the east coast. (**5 marks**)

(c) • Image has a responsibility to pay its **employees** a fair wage – at least the minimum – and have good working conditions in the factory. (**4 marks**) They 'employ seventy workers in a large factory' and paying a fair wage to them will add to the firm's costs. (**2 marks**)

• The firm also has a social responsibility to the local **community** in which it operates. This may involve sponsoring a local event or team. (**4 marks**) Image has 'a large factory in an industrial estate'. Perhaps they should sponsor a local soccer team, which will cost them in the short term but will bring long-term benefits. (**2 marks**)

• Firms have social responsibilities to their **customers**. This involves treating them with respect and dealing with any complaints they may have. (**4 marks**) Image 'sells mainly to paint and DIY shops'. It should give occasional discounts and special offers to its customers. (**2 marks**)

• All firms have responsibilities to protect the environment. This involves correct **dumping** and disposal of waste materials. (**4 marks**) This is especially important for a business like Image, which would be dealing with some chemical and perhaps toxic waste. This will add to the firm's costs. (**2 marks**)

• Firms that are environmentally responsible should use materials that can be recycled and also **recycle** any waste materials. (**4 marks**) This may involve Image setting up a recycling facility at the factory. (**2 marks**)